Sounds & Words
Supporting language learning through phonics

Lynn Erler and Julie Prince

Other titles in the CfBT Education Trust publications catalogue:

Young Pathfinders

This popular series is full of stimulating and practical ideas to help teach languages to young children. Whether you are a specialist language teacher or not, you're sure to find something to inspire you.

Games & fun activities (YPF2)
Cynthia Martin

Are you sitting comfortably? (YPF3)
Telling stories to young language learners
Daniel Tierney and **Patricia Dobson**

First steps to reading and writing (YPF5)
Preparation for reading and writing
Christina Skarbek

Let's join in! (YPF6)
Rhymes, poems and songs
Cynthia Martin and **Catherine Cheater**

Making the link (YPF7)
Relating languages to other work in the school
Daniel Tierney and **Malcolm Hope**

The literacy link (YPF9)
Catherine Cheater and **Anne Farren**

A world of languages (YPF10)
Developing children's love of languages
Manjula Datta and **Cathy Pomphrey**

A flying start! (YPF11)
Introducing early language learning
June de Silva and **Peter Satchwell**

Working together (YPF12)
Native speaker assistants in the primary school
Cynthia Martin and **Anne Farren**

Mind the gap! (YPF13)
Improving transition between Key Stage 2 and 3
Rosemary Bevis and **Ann Gregory**

Speak up! (YPF15)
Getting talking in the languages classroom
Peter Satchwell with **June de Silva**

Leading the way (YPF16)
Coordinating primary languages
Bernadette Clinton and **Marion Vincent**

My Languages Portfolio
(to be published in 2012)
Based on earlier versions of the Junior European Languages Portfolio (ELP), this new version of the learner self-assessment tool offers an explicit model for progression in language learning from Year 3 to Year 6. Teachers can select from over 40 attractive activity pages to encourage children to evaluate and celebrate their progress and to create a portfolio of their achievements. A detailed Teacher Guide explains the rationale for activities and offers suggestions for classroom exploitation. Activity pages are available on the CD-ROM in electronic format so teachers can adapt content to suit classes and individual children.

For more information on these and other titles available from CfBT Education Trust, contact:
education@cfbt.com

» Contents

Introduction — 3

Chapter 1 Identifying and producing phonemes — 11

Chapter 2 Distinguishing between phonemes — 25

Chapter 3 Phoneme–grapheme correspondence — 31

Chapter 4 Decoding and synthesising — 41

Language support: French, Spanish and German — 65

Acknowledgements

The authors are grateful to many people who have been instrumental to our work and the ideas in this book. In the first instance, we wish to thank all the children and teachers we have taught and worked with over the years, who have tried out our resources and teaching ideas. In particular we are indebted to the staff and children of Hawkedon Primary School and the head teacher, Alan Youd. We are very grateful to photographer Nigel Bird, who is responsible for the photography throughout the book.

Lynn expresses her gratitude to her family and particularly her brother Jeff, whose struggles with English phonics as a child were 'miraculously' offset by his ease as an 8 year old with decoding French, which gave her the idea in the first place. Thank you especially to Steffen and Janine who introduced her to French phonics via their beginner reader *Nounourse et Ses Amis* at primary school in France.

Julie is indebted to her family for their understanding and patience during the writing of this book. Her children, Helena and Anthony, tried out many of the activities before they were used in the classroom while her husband, David, is now more familiar with the phonemes of three European languages and their IPA symbols than he ever expected to be!

Bibliography

Cheater, C. and Farren, A. (2001) *The literacy link*, London: CILT.

Pagniez-Delbert, T. (1995) *Á l'Écoute des Sons – Les Voyelles,* Paris: CLE International.

Price, G. (2005, revised edition) *An Introduction to French Pronunciation,* Malden MA, Oxford: Blackwell Publishing.

Sewell, P. (2009) *La prononciation française pour de vrai* (set of 3 DVDs), London: Penny Sewell and Birkbeck University of London.

The International Phonetic Association (1999) *Handbook of the International Phonetic Association*, Cambridge: Cambridge University Press.

» Introduction

This book is about developing children's perception (identification) and production of the sounds of the foreign language which they are learning. It presents the phoneme–grapheme correspondences of three of the foreign languages which children learn at primary level – French, Spanish and German.

- Phonemes are the individual sounds of a language, for instance the sound of 'm' is a phoneme made by putting the lips together and making a humming sound.
- The grapheme which corresponds to that sound in English (and in French, Spanish and German) is the letter 'm' or 'M', or it could be 'mm' in the middle of a word.

The key purposes of this book are:
- to support the children's progress with phonemes and graphemes in the foreign language;
- to guide and support foreign language teachers who are non-language specialists to develop their own understanding of, and mastery over, the phonics rules and pronunciation.

Most Key Stage 2 children understand that graphemes on a page represent sounds, and that a string of graphemes together with a space before and after the string represents a word, with its sounds and its meaning.

They are also aware that they might be able to divide the word into segments or syllables, roughly related to the phoneme divisions. The focus on phonemes and their graphemes is called phonics work, which children in Key Stage 1 develop a familiarity with because understanding spelling-to-sound rules in any language is a basic skill needed for learning to read. For most children decoding the graphemes of a word to discover its phonemes allows them to access the meaning of the word.

Research in language learning and memory capacity has shown that knowing how to say a word in a foreign language helps the learner to be able to:
- repeat the sounds in his or her head to memorise them and store them in long-term memory;
- say the sounds correctly when sub-vocalising or practising them in his or her head;
- rehearse the sounds to get them right before speaking them out loud;
- remember the meaning of the word when hearing it again some other time;
- repeat the sounds of something someone has said in order to be sure of the meaning.

In short, we now know from research what we may unconsciously know from common sense: that being able to say words correctly and to hear the sounds of words correctly in your head is a vital element when learning vocabulary, and for reading, writing, speaking and listening comprehension.

Many people believe that children pick up foreign languages without much effort, but usually such children live in an environment where they hear the foreign language most of every day and have to use it to communicate with the people around them. That is not the case in our schools however much we may try to make the foreign language alive and present in the school. Even for the most confident and receptive child, a lesson or so a week is not enough to remember and use much of the foreign language easily. Learning how to decode the sounds of words from their written forms, however, can provide an enormous support for the language learner.

The child can:
- use the sounds to help remember the word(s);
- feel confident that he or she can use the phoneme–grapheme system of the foreign language to be able to say any word seen in that language;
- use written words, for instance in lists or poems, to practise saying the words in his/her head or aloud with the knowledge that he or she can decode correctly;
- rehearse new words correctly until they are stored securely in long-term memory;
- recognise words when he or she hears them or sees them in new contexts;
- feel competent as a foreign language learner and user.

It is important that these aspects of learning the foreign language are acquired by the child early on. Phonics knowledge helps develop the child's positive self-concept as a foreign language learner and sets him or her on a path well motivated for further learning with the expectation of success.

Note that we have written this book with primary teachers and children in mind. However, the approach and many of the resources and activities have been used successfully – and to the enjoyment of both teachers and learners – with 11–16 year-olds. In fact, often very little adaptation is needed and older learners are so grateful finally to get control over their pronunciation and decoding!

» Perception and production

Perception

This book will guide you as the teacher to help children listen to and recognise individual sounds and groups of sounds in the foreign language. Children will also learn about the letters and letter strings in the foreign language which represent the sounds. Children will learn to perceive specific sounds as parts of syllables and words. This book offers a variety of activities for practising the perception of sounds through hearing and through seeing the graphemes.

Production

This book will support you as the foreign language teacher to help your learners to produce the phonemes of the foreign language when they see the graphemes that represent those sounds either as parts of words, whole words or words in the context of a song, poem, play or story. Children will have opportunities to **repeat** sounds after hearing them and to **produce** sounds when they see the graphemes in the foreign language.

Examples for perception and production activities are given throughout this book in the three languages. In addition, resources for teaching, practising and assessment in French, Spanish and German appear in the **Language support** section at the end of the book and on the accompanying CD.

» Users of this book

As stated above, this book can be used with learners of practically all ages. It is a resource for the teacher who:
- may never have explicitly learned the phonics and phoneme-grapheme system of the language;
- although competent with the language has not yet put together a full phonics teaching programme;
- notices children struggling and would like some guidance on how to identify and address the problem/s;
- is not a specialist in the language and needs support in learning it.

Recordings of phonemes, syllables, words, sentences, songs and poems, together with the PowerPoint presentations on pronunciation, can be used by the teacher for their foreign language development as well as for classroom work with the children.

The book is constructed sequentially, beginning with listening and hearing sounds and moving on from there, following a progression based on the Key Stage 2 Framework for Languages, that is found in first language literacy teaching, for instance in the Primary Framework for Literacy. Secondary MFL teachers in England will recognise the progression we present here as the same as that found in the Attainment Target Levels for the language skills.

Sounds & Words – Supporting language learning through phonics

» Progression

The progression throughout this book is based on the learners' progress in phonic skills, starting, in Chapter 1, with recognising particular phonemes when heard and then being able to say the phonemes themselves. From there the children progress to being able to hear the difference between two similar phonemes, for which activities are suggested in Chapter 2. In Chapter 3 we move on to matching the phonemes to written letters and letter strings and finally, in Chapter 4, the learners progress to using their phonic skills to help them read and write words, phrases and sentences. The rate at which children progress will vary between year groups and even between individual learners (which is why we have included support and extension suggestions for each activity). With older children (Year 5 upwards) you will be able to progress more quickly but, if this is the first time you have done phonics work with them, we still suggest you begin with some of the activities in Chapter 1 to ensure the foundations are in place.

Activities throughout this book are linked to the learning objectives from the Key Stage 2 Framework for Languages. This non-statutory guidance was published in 2005 as part of the National Languages Strategy.

As we have said, in terms of developing the children's phonic skills, you will generally move through the book in order, using the activities in Chapter 1 with beginners and progressing to Chapter 4 when the children are ready to start writing words and phrases. However, there are some exceptions. You could, for example, focus on a small number of phonemes such as 'a' [a], 'i' [i] and 'o' [o] in French, help the children practise saying them and then show them the corresponding letters (that is, letters 'a', 'i' and 'o'; no alternatives at this stage). You could then ask the children to read some simple syllables such as 'ma', 'ti' and 'lo', as suggested at the beginning of Chapter 4. They may also be able to write similar syllables if you say them clearly and slowly. This decoding and synthesising could include very simple words such as *'moto'* or *'papa'*. How exciting for absolute beginners, after learning just three phonemes, to be able to write real words! You could do this each time you have focused on a phoneme, or several phonemes, and, of course, once you have made sure the children can hear the sounds, pronounce them and link each one to a corresponding grapheme. However, there will still be a general progression from Chapter 1 to Chapter 4 and children will need to be familiar with most of the common phonemes and their corresponding graphemes (including alternatives, such as 'au' [o] in French) before they are ready for most of the reading and writing activities we describe in Chapter 4.

By Chapter 4, the children have been introduced to almost all the common phonemes in French and their corresponding graphemes. They have been introduced to alternative graphemes for one phoneme (e.g. 'o', 'au' and 'eau') and silent letters. They should be able to read aloud phonetically-regular words and phrases and use their phonic knowledge to write simple words and phrases. They should also be able to listen to a spoken text and follow it in the written version. These skills correspond to the KS2 Framework objectives for Year 4, based on the assumption that that is the children's second year of study. In other words, it will probably have taken you two years to get to this point in French.

Years 5 and 6 children will build on these skills, continuing to use the activities from Chapter 4. This may be the time you choose to introduce the less common phonemes such as [ɲ] (as in *'montagne'*) and [ij] (as in *'vanille'*). In Year 5 you will probably also concentrate on dictionary skills, as outlined in the KS2 Framework objectives for Year 5. There are activities for this in Chapter 4. By the end of Year 4 the children have 'covered the basics' in terms of their phonic knowledge and Years 5 and 6 can be spent developing those skills and building up reading and writing skills. You will be focused mainly on Chapter 4 activities but revisiting earlier chapters as necessary when you have identified a particular problem area for some children.

If you are teaching children who are perhaps in their third or fourth year of study but who have done no previous phonics work, you will be able to progress more quickly as you will already be doing reading and writing activities with them. For example, you could use some of the activities from Chapter 3 (such as the Phoneme–Grapheme Running Game) as diagnostic tools to identify which correspondences the children need help with and also which phonemes they need help pronouncing. You will also need to include some activities from Chapter 1 to check the children are able to pick out phonemes in spoken texts. By using a simple activity such as the card-reading

Introduction

activity from Chapter 4 you will be able to identify whether the children are confusing some phonemes (such as 'ou' and 'u'), in which case some of the activities in Chapter 2 will be useful. In this way, you will already be doing literacy work with children who have been studying the language for two years or more, and will be using Chapter 4 to support this but, if the children have never done any phonics work, you will also be using Chapters 1–3 to ensure they have the necessary basic knowledge and skills to support their reading and writing.

» Accompanying resources

Specific teaching resources accompany many of the activities in this book, highlighted in bold. These might be printable resources in French, German or Spanish or they might be audio material containing sections and exercises for work on individual sounds. There are also other resources containing printable materials that can be adapted as well as a number of PowerPoint presentations which will help develop practice in producing the phonemes.

The listening material progresses from single sounds to words, phrases and sentences containing the focus sound. This resource is essential for the non-specialist who needs practice listening and producing the phonemes.

The most useful part of the audio section for non-specialists is **Recording: Individual Phonemes**, which contains recordings of individual phonemes in French, Spanish and German. You can use these for your own training, listening to and repeating them and checking that you know the corresponding letter(s). You can also use them as a resource in class. Whenever an activity requires the children to listen to a phoneme, you have the option of playing the recording rather than saying it yourself.

For the same reason we have also included other recordings that you can use in this way. For example, if you are doing the Silly Syllables activity from the end of Chapter 3 you can use **Recording: Recognising Syllables**, which contains individual syllables recorded in the three languages.

Key Phoneme Guides

The Key Phoneme Guides for French, Spanish and German start on page 67. These guides provide a quick and handy reference to phonemes which are most likely to need explicit teaching to the children. The guides are not comprehensive or exhaustive, from a strictly phonetic point of view. We have put the guides together based on sounds in words which the children are likely to meet and to give a brief overview of the phonics systems of the three languages. Each guide shows the written letter or letter string, the International Phonetic Association symbol, if possible any similar sound in English along with an English word that contains the sound, and a key word in the foreign language. From the guides **Individual Phonemes** are recorded. Certain key phonemes appear in some resources with long and short vowel sounds conflated: on the **PowerPoint** presentations and in the **Sounds and Spellings Support Sheets**.

» Links with literacy

The Independent Review of the Primary Curriculum (2009) reinforced the importance of linking literacy work and foreign language learning. Indeed, it recommended that languages be situated within the area of 'Understanding English, Communication and Languages' so that teachers could exploit links between the two.

'Developing language in the primary school: Literacy and primary languages', published by the DfES in 2009, set out how the key objectives of the Primary Framework for Literacy and the Key Stage 2 Framework for Languages are aligned and mutually supportive.

Phonics teaching has been well established in primary schools, especially since the National Literacy Hour was introduced in 1999. The use of the systematic synthetic phonics method for teaching reading has been given an extra focus since the change in government in 2010, with the introduction of a new, statutory phonics screening check for all pupils in Year 1 from June 2012. The objectives in the KS2 Framework for Languages include a specific focus on phonics in language learning, as do the non-statutory schemes of work for KS2 French, Spanish and German, published in 2007 by the QCA.

The approach to teaching sound-spelling relationships in foreign languages which we take in this book draws principally on synthetic phonics using word segmentation, identifying and blending phonemes. However, we also include aspects of analytic phonics, in that we make use of rhymes and spelling by analogy.

Though this book concentrates on the sounds of individual letters, letter strings and syllables, where whole words are presented it is important that they are linked to their meanings either through objects, pictures, demonstrations or translations.

This book has close links to the *The literacy link* (Young Pathfinder 9) by Catherine Cheater and Anne Farren published in 2001 by CILT, the National Centre for Languages and available from CfBT Education Trust. In *The literacy link* phonics work in English is linked to similar work in the foreign languages and a variety of activities at word, sentence and text levels is offered. You may wish to combine work in this book with that found in *The literacy link*.

We focus in this book more intensely on the foreign language phonics themselves by providing:
- explanations;
- learner activities at the various literacy levels;
- support and extension for activities;
- assessment opportunities.

The activities are all backed up by a wide range of resources including:
- Worksheets;
- Key Phoneme Guides with pronunciations and spellings for each of the three languages;
- PowerPoint presentations;
- Templates for copying and use in other languages;
- Games;
- Links to audio recordings with pronunciation of key phonemes.

» Using the activities in this book

In order to be sure that children have been introduced to, practised and learned all the key phonemes of the language, we strongly urge you to keep a record of what you have done, if it is only to tick off each phoneme. In the resources you will find each phoneme represented as:
- a single sound;
- spellings (graphemes) of the sound;
- the sound in single words, in songs, poems, sentences.

Although you can use this book to 'dip into' you need to dip with an informed purpose which we will explain below. However, we suggest that you first of all familiarise yourself with the progression that is present in the flow of Chapters 1 to 4. Read the introduction to each chapter to understand what level or aspect of phonics you will encounter.

You may choose to follow a programme with a small group of phonemes which looks like this progression in phonemic knowledge and skill development:
- hear, identify;
- repeat, produce;
- link spelling to sound;
- decode, speak and write at word, phrase, sentence level.

Alternatively, you can dip into the book, once you have identified the learners' phonemic problem/s: which phoneme is causing them a problem. The learners themselves can help you identify their difficulties, if you ask them. In any case observe them carefully to find out:
- Can they hear the sound and distinguish it when it comes up?
- Can they repeat, mimic, produce the sound?
- Can they decode the letter, letter string, word correctly? (By 'correctly' we mean a reasonable approximation such that it is not frustrating the child or impeding learning or progress.)
- Do they need additional practice in order to master hearing, saying, decoding, or spelling the sound?

Then choose the chapter that is appropriate to your learner's or learners' area of need. Select activities which are most suited to your learner/s, your setting and circumstances. Vary whole-class with small group and pairwork activities, if possible, and keep track of what you have worked on with the children.

The structure and purpose of many activities in this book will be familiar to primary teachers, and to their children from other lessons in school, particularly literacy lessons. For additional activities you can draw and adapt from your own experience and other literature. You can always ask the children to suggest their favourite ways of honing their skills.

Embedded in all phonics work is the fact that some children learn more rapidly than others and some classes or children need more revisiting than others. Children can help each other, if directed carefully and the right atmosphere exists in the class. Spot checks on knowledge of a phoneme or phoneme–grapheme link may mean going back to an activity where children can become the lead once they have mastered the knowledge or skill. You will soon recognise the favourite activities which children will be eager to do, sometimes as a 'quickie' just before break or going home.

» Assessment

Assessing the children's phonic skills should form part of your normal assessment, whether it is formal or informal and by the teacher, peer or individual. Opportunities are flagged with '**Progress Check**' alongside an activity that provides a good point at which to assess the children's abilities and learning. To help you record the children's progress you might like to use the **Teacher's Phonics Goals Progress Chart** (see **Resource: Teacher's Phonics Goals Progress Chart**). There is also a set of **Can-Do Statements** (see **Resource: Learner's Can-Do Statements**), based on the objectives of the KS2 Framework, for the children to use.

» International Phonetic Association

Throughout the book we use symbols from the International Phonetic Association (IPA) in square brackets [ ]. It is not widely used in the UK but it is used in dictionaries and we have found it the most consistent way to describe a particular sound in this book. For example, the letter 'u' in French makes a sound that does not exist in English. Its IPA symbol is [y]. To check sounds and symbols, refer to the Key Phoneme Guides at the back of the book. We suggest that you do not use the IPA symbols with the children.

» Confusions with English

Year 3 teachers sometimes express concerns that phonics in the foreign language may confuse children who have not yet mastered the phoneme–grapheme rules in English. However, this is not a reason to avoid phonics work in the foreign language. Activities such as comparing and contrasting languages (e.g. French and English) and making explicit reference to the differences can help reinforce literacy work rather than undermine it. The Key Stage 2 Framework for Languages included literacy work from Year 3; therefore avoiding phonics in the foreign language denies children the opportunity to take on important skills for helping them start to read and write in the foreign language. Rather than avoiding phonics in the foreign language we suggest special activities to make the contrasts between English and the foreign language more explicit. We have found that children really enjoy these activities, such as 'Arguing Football Stars' (see page 32).

» Supporting struggling children

For some children the concept that letters on a page represent sounds can be difficult to grasp. Sometimes this problem arises because of the arbitrariness of the spelling system of English. There are a great number of rules and exceptions to rules for changing graphemes to phonemes in English which is known for its opaqueness of spelling-to-sound correspondences.

The foreign languages presented in this book have more transparent phoneme–grapheme and grapheme–phoneme systems than English, so the rules for transforming letters and letter strings to sounds in these languages are more readily understood and learned. Occasionally a child who struggles with English spellings-to-sounds will pick up the rules for phonics in the foreign language quickly and successfully. Often these children can transfer their new sense of competency to support their work in English!

However, for a very few children phonics work in the foreign language only confuses them further. Please be aware of such children and their struggles and make your judgement as to the extent of their participation in the activities in this book. Most activities should be accessible for all, but some exercises may be difficult for a few children to feel comfortable with and to benefit from.

Teachers sometimes ask about the order in which to present or focus on phonemes. A good approach is to focus first on the foreign language phonemes that you feel most comfortable with. It is logical to focus on phonemes that come up with the words that you are teaching, for example, the 'u' of 'salut' or the 'on' and the 'ou' of 'bonjour'. A systematic approach to phonics in any language is, in the long run, more useful to the children. We have, therefore, devised this book to present phonemes in a coherent and consistent fashion, while allowing you, the teacher, flexibility in terms of order, presentation and re-visiting for reinforcement, and we hope you enjoy the activities as much as the children will.

» Chapter outlines

Chapters 1 to 4 are outlined below showing the built-in progression in learning identified above. Sometimes we have needed to skip forward to decoding, for instance we touch on it already in Chapter 1. On the whole the chapters follow the natural sequence for learning any language mirrored in the Primary Framework for Literacy, and the lower Attainment Target Levels in secondary-level foreign language learning.

Chapter 1
Identifying and producing phonemes
This chapter introduces key phonemes, focusing on those different from English, and presents ideas for activities based on identifying specific sounds (e.g. in songs and rhymes). The activities are particularly linked to the **Year 3 Oracy** objectives of the KS2 Framework for Languages. We also begin to introduce sound–letter (phoneme–grapheme) correspondences (rules) in the foreign language.

Chapter 2
Distinguishing between phonemes
This chapter introduces further key phonemes that are more difficult (e.g. the French nasal sounds) or less common. There are also ideas for activities based on hearing and producing the difference between two similar sounds (e.g. for 'u' and 'ou' in French), including the role of accents. This chapter especially links to the **Year 4 Oracy** objectives from the Framework.

Chapter 3
Phoneme–grapheme correspondence
This chapter concentrates on how the key phonemes are represented in written form, including letter strings that make a single phoneme, and suggests ideas for classroom activities to help children practise making these links. Activities support the Framework objectives particularly for the **Literacy strand** in **Years 3 and 4.**

Sounds & Words – Supporting language learning through phonics

Chapter 4
Decoding and synthesising

This chapter focuses on skills that will help children improve their reading and writing in the foreign language, such as breaking down words into individual phonemes and synthesising words from individual phonemes. These are skills they will have been taught in their own language in KS1 and complement the Primary Framework for Literacy. There is further work at word and then sentence level.

Language support

This is a reference section and includes information that is specific to each language – French, Spanish and German. The chapter includes:
- a list of the key phonemes in each language;
- stress and intonation in each language;
- examples of words in each language for each key phoneme;
- Spanish stress rules;
- key rules for silent letters;
- the sounds and spellings of French, Spanish and German.

The Key Phoneme Guides section has been designed for the teacher to have a complete overview of the phonics system of the language in order to be sure that each child has learned the whole system.

The **Learner's Can-Do Statements** are for the learner (and teacher) to track the learning. You as the teacher may have, or wish to devise, your own way for being certain that each learner has a complete set of phonic knowledge.

Chapter 1
» Identifying and producing phonemes

Topics covered in this chapter

Activities for hearing and identifying phonemes

Activities for producing phonemes and links to graphemes

Rhyming

Introducing syllables

Support for non-language specialists

This chapter focuses first on helping children to **hear** the new phonemes in their new foreign language. It is easy to assume that anyone can hear the individual foreign language sounds when listening to or singing a song, for instance. However, that may not be the case and often it is not. By the age of four our brains have structured 'sound categories' for the sounds of our mother tongue to the exclusion of other irrelevant sounds (unless a second language is also learned that early). We may not actually hear other sounds. The activities for developing listening and hearing skills can be used with any year group. If a learner is having difficulties with speaking, spelling, reading or listening, it is important to check that he or she can hear the sounds.

Activities to practise **saying** phonemes are included toward the end of the chapter and we **introduce decoding** phonemes from graphemes according to the phoneme–grapheme correspondence rules of the language. There will be a greater focus on this in Chapter 3. If you are a non-specialist teacher, there is further guidance at the end of this chapter on page 23.

We see, then, that one of the key skills that children must practise in their first year of language study is hearing individual sounds (phonemes) in another language. Some of the sounds will be the same as or very similar to English. Of these, some will be represented in the foreign language by the same letter(s) as in English and some will be represented by different letters (e.g. the 'sh' sound in French is represented by the letters 'ch'), i.e. they have a **different** phoneme–grapheme correspondence.

Other sounds will be different from English sounds and children will need particular practice in hearing and imitating these sounds (e.g. the French 'u' [y] sound as in 'tu'). Throughout the book we use the symbols of the International Phonetic Association (IPA) shown in square brackets [ ] to represent sounds, as we have found it the most consistent way to describe a particular sound. While this is not widely used in the UK, it is found in dictionaries. For example, the letter 'u' in French makes a sound that does not exist in English. To represent the sound we have used its IPA symbol: [y]. To check sounds and symbols, refer to the **Key Phoneme Guides** on page 67 and the audio version **Recording: Individual Phonemes** on the accompanying CD.

Developing new sound categories

By the age of four a child's brain has developed what are called 'sound categories' for the sounds in their first language. Older children may not be able to hear or easily identify new or different sounds that do not exist in their mother tongue sound categories and, in the KS2 classroom, developing new sound categories is done most rapidly and securely by means of explicit, consistent teaching, and practice such as we present in this book. A normally developing child is fully able to develop new sound categories – think of the many bilingual children in the UK!

Sounds & Words – Supporting language learning through phonics

» KS2 Framework links

Activities in this chapter help children practise hearing phonemes. This skill links with the KS2 Framework for Languages:

O3.2 Recognise and respond to sound patterns and words
- Listen with care
- Identify phonemes which are the same as or different from English and other known languages
- Speak clearly and confidently

The second bullet point above is important. There may be children in your class who speak another language and they may find that some of the sounds in the language you are teaching also occur in the other language(s) they know, but perhaps not in English (e.g. the Gaelic 'ch' as in 'loch' and Spanish 'j'). The rest of the class will find this interesting and these children may even be able to act as models when you are practising pronunciation, although asking children to demonstrate sounds must, of course, be handled sensitively.

» Activities for hearing and identifying phonemes

Before you begin, you may want to familiarise yourself with the **Key Phoneme Guides** for French, Spanish and/or German (see page 67). Audio versions of the individual phonemes are available (**Recording: Individual Phonemes**) and we suggest that the best way to get started is to select the phoneme/s you wish to teach and practise with the children first.

If you feel unsure about the phonics of the language, listen to the recordings of the individual phonemes and repeat the sounds. There are lists of words by phoneme (**Resource** and **Recording: Example Words by Phoneme**) and lists of words by syllable count (**Resource** and **Recording: Words by Syllable Count**) which you can also listen to and repeat. Watch your mouth in the mirror as you do so. Really exercise those muscles. Test yourself by reading the sound and word first and then listening to it.

Same as English or Different?

This activity will help the children tune into sounds that may be new to them. In the case of sounds that are only slightly different from English (such as the French 'ou' [u]) it will build the foundations for good pronunciation from the start.

Let the children hear a sound from the suggested sounds listed below (spoken by you or selected from the recorded sound files). For each sound they hear they must decide if it occurs in English or not. The children can respond in various ways such as clapping or waving if the sound is the same as English, or performing two different actions such as nodding or shaking their head. You could make the activity even more fun by turning it into a running game, in the hall or playground, getting the children to run between two walls or posts designated as 'like English' and 'not like English'. Make sure that after each run the children all gather back around you in the centre so they hear the next sound clearly. Suggested sounds are:

	Like English	**Different from English**
French	oi [wa] (*oiseau*, wagon), e [ə] (*le*, the), è [ɛ] (*belle*, vet), ch [ʃ] (*chat*, shoe)	u [y], an [ɑ̃], in [ɛ̃], on [ɔ̃], un [œ̃]
Spanish	z [θ], c(e/i) [θ] (*cinco*, think), d [ð] (*nada*, although), au [au] (*aunque*, cow), oi/oy [oi] (*voy*, toy)	j [x], g(e/i) [x], rr [rr]
German	u [u], z [ts], äu [oi] u [u] (*du*, boot), z [ts] (*zu*, cats), äu [oi] (*Mäuse*, toy)	ö [ø:], ü [y], ch [ç], r [r] and [ʁ], pf [pf], zw [tsv]

Support

Let the children hear more sounds, either spoken by you or from the recorded sound file **(Recording: Same as English or Different?)**, and determine whether they are the same in English or different from English. Start with the phonemes that are most obviously different from English such as 'j' in Spanish or a nasal sound in French, such as 'on'. Really emphasise the sound if children are finding it difficult. Children will watch their peers and use them for support if unsure.

Extension

Gradually move on to sounds that are difficult to make such as 'u' in French and those that are quite similar to English such as the French 'é' (see **Recording: Individual Phonemes**) which does not have a diphthong 'a-ee-yuh' as it usually does in English.

Pass the Object

This activity links to framework objective:

O3.2 Recognise and respond to sound patterns and words

In this activity, children listen to a rhyme, poem or song (**Resource** and **Recording: Songs and Rhymes**) and listen out for a particular phoneme. When the children first listen for a particular sound you might like to start with one that is the same as in English such as 'th' for learners of Spanish or 'ei' for learners of German. This will get the children used to listening for specific sounds and responding in a certain way. You can then progress to listening for sounds that are different from English, such as 'u' [y] for learners of French.

Get the children to sit in a circle in groups of about six to eight and give them an object – a small ball, teddy, or something related to the song. Tell the children which sound they will be listening for and that each time they hear that sound the person holding the object must pass it to the person on their left.

As an alternative to using an object you could ask the children to make a gesture, such as putting their hands on their head to show that they have heard the sound. This is especially useful in songs where the sound is repeated very quickly and the children are struggling to pass the object in time. This type of response is easier for you to assess as you can watch the children carefully and see who is responding quickly and who is hesitant or having to follow their peers. The children may be able to suggest other ways of responding such as clapping or waving. Similar activities are suggested on page 10 of *The literacy link* (CILT 2001).

Support

If some children are finding the activity difficult, make sure you are near them during the song so that you can sing along and emphasise the sound each time it occurs.

Extension

Sometimes you will find a song, rhyme or poem that contains many examples of a particular sound with frequent repetitions. These types of songs make the activity more challenging and often more fun as the children have to be very quick. You will have to judge whether the speed of a recording is too fast and, if so, you might have to sing the song yourself or ask a native speaker to record it for you at a slower pace.

Revisiting

You can revisit this activity over time (including with Year 6, and also older learners) as the children become more proficient. Gradually introduce more challenging songs, perhaps with a quicker pace or a sound that is harder to distinguish from another (e.g. French 'u' versus 'ou'). Very able children can be further challenged by being given two different phonemes to listen out for at the same time in a sentence or song, for instance.

Songs to practise specific phonemes

Recording: Songs and Rhymes

Here are some examples of songs and rhymes recorded on the CD that are useful for practising particular sounds.

French

é [e]	Il était un petit navire
i [i]	La fête à la souris; Au pays de lundi
ou [u]	Dans la forêt lointaine; Loup y es-tu ?
o/au [o]	Les petits poissons; Il était un petit navire; Bateau, ciseau
u [y]	Une poule sur un mur
an/en [ɑ̃]	Vive le vent (tune of Jingle Bells)
in [ɛ̃]	Ragotin; Le petit lapin; Un petit bonhomme au bout du chemin
on [ɔ̃]	Sur le pont d'Avignon
j [ʒ]	Il était un petit navire (first verse)
r [ʀ]	Am stram gram

Spanish

e [e]	Lero, lero, candelero
i [i]	Debajo un botón
j [x]	José se llamaba el padre; Había una vieja
ll [ʎ]	Centellea Estrellita
rr [rr]	Arre borriquito; El perro de San Roque

German

ä [ɛ], ei [aɪ]	Ein Männlein steht im Walde
pf, ch [ç], o [ɔ]	Hopp, hopp, hopp
ö [ø:], zw [zv], tsch [tʃ]	Alle Vögel sind schon da
ö [ø:], ä [ɛ], sch [ʃ], ch [ç]	Alle meine Entchen
ch [ç], ie, ei, ü, ö	Summ, summ, summ
zt, tz, ü, ä, ckch [kç]	Es tanzt ein Bi-Ba-Butzemann
Vowels	Hänsel und Gretel
Crisp consonants	Kuckuck, Kuckuck

Further songs and rhymes that are useful for practising particular sounds can be found on several teaching resources websites such as www.momes.net and www.comptines.net. Examples include: Léon le caméléon, À la queue leu leu, Le kangourou, Gouttes gouttelettes de pluie, Mon chapeau. You can also ask your Foreign Language Assistant or another native speaker for their song or rhyme suggestions.

Phoneme Towers

This activity is a progression from the previous one as it places more importance on trying to hear every instance that the phoneme occurs in the song.

Once the children have become fairly confident in identifying a particular sound you could progress to asking them to count how many times they hear that sound in a particular passage, song or rhyme. Again, this may be a useful assessment tool. Children can work individually, in pairs or in groups of three. They could simply use a tally system on a mini whiteboard but there's also scope for making this activity more fun and more tactile by using small objects such as counters, play balls or multilink cubes. As a team the children must take an object each time they hear the designated phoneme. If multilink cubes are used the children can build them into a tower. The following example, 'Vive le Vent' (from the CD or reading it aloud yourself) is listening for the sound 'an' [ã].

Vive le Vent

Sur le long chemin
Tout blanc de neige blanche
Un vieux monsieur s'avance
Sa canne dans la main
Et tout là-haut le vent
Qui siffle dans les branches
Lui souffle la romance
Qu'il chantait petit enfant

(Chorus)
Vive le vent, vive le vent
Vive le vent d'hiver
Qui s'en va sifflant, soufflant
Dans les grands sapins verts
Vive le temps, vive le temps
Vive le temps d'hiver
Boules de neige et jour de l'an
Et bonne année grand-mère!

The phoneme 'an' [ã] (written as 'an', 'am', 'en' or 'em') occurs 11 times in the first verse and 13 times in the chorus.

The children will need to hear the song about three times. Once they have created their tower, one per team, they can check it when they listen again. Finally the groups can compare the height of their towers, count and say how many cubes they have. You can then provide the correct answer. If the children are within a few cubes of the correct answer they have done very well. Let them know that they do not have to have the exact number to have succeeded at this task.

Support
As this is a group activity there is the opportunity for peer support. If it becomes too difficult for the children to listen and build a tower simultaneously then just get them to make a simple tally. If the music is too fast you could try singing it at a slower pace. This also allows you to place emphasis on the key phoneme when it occurs. If you don't feel confident singing then pause the music frequently.

Extension
More able children will enjoy the challenge of trying to spot the exact number of times the phoneme occurs but do explain to all the children that they have succeeded in the task if they have heard the phoneme **most** of the time.

Revisiting
With older children, or those who have already been introduced to phoneme–grapheme correspondences, you might prefer to give them a transcript of the song and ask them to highlight the graphemes 'an/am/en/em' [ã] as a means of checking their answers at the end. You will need to draw their attention to 'canne' and 'année', which do not contain the phoneme 'an'. The children might be able to suggest why these are different (they contain double 'n'). Children who have learned or are learning to read in English are used to 'exceptions'!

» Activities for producing phonemes and links to graphemes

Phoneme imitation and mimes
As well as **identifying** sounds when they hear them, the children will also need plenty of practice **producing** the sounds, repeating them after you or after a native speaker. Let the children simply listen to the sound several times before they start repeating it, to allow everyone a chance to hear the sound correctly. The CD has several exercises which are useful for this. See **Recording: Individual Phonemes**.

The next step is for the children to echo the sound after you. They can start doing this as a whole class but eventually you will need to hear them group by group or even individually to check they are producing the sound correctly. To ensure everyone is heard, the children can stand in a circle and throw a ball to each other. The person who catches the ball must say the sound and then sit down. To introduce an element of fun you could time how long it takes to get round the whole class and for everyone to be sitting down. Next lesson try to beat your record! 'Pass the Parcel' can also be used for this.

A way of making this skill more multi-sensory is to ask the children to invent whole-body mimes for the different sounds they are practising. Start by giving them some examples and then allow them time in groups to get creative with their own mimes. Encourage them to listen very carefully to each sound and imagine what that sound would look like – is it long or short, fat or thin, soft or sharp? For example, in German 'o' [o:] as in 'rot' might sound round and fat whereas the 'ü' [y:] of 'grün' sounds wide and drawn-out. In French the sound 'ou' [u] can sound soft and relaxed as if sighing whereas 'u' [y] suggests a much shorter and sharper gesture. In Spanish the 'j' [x] sound might suggest a growling animal to the children whereas the sound 'i' [i] might be perceived as small and cute (mouse-like).

Linking phonemes and graphemes
In their first year of language study, which for most will be Year 3, children also need to start relating sounds to spelling patterns in the new language, once they know the phonemes well. This relates to the following Year 3 literacy objective:

L3.2 Make links between some phonemes, rhymes and spellings, and read aloud familiar words.

Even if the sound is one that also occurs in English it might be represented by a different letter or letters in the language being studied, in other words the phoneme–grapheme correspondence may be different. For example, the French sound 'ch' [ʃ] also occurs in English but we write it as 'sh' rather than 'ch' as it is written in French. In Spanish the sound 'th' [θ] is represented by the letter 'z' or a soft 'c' (before 'e' or 'i') but in English, of course, it is written 'th'.

Introducing the link between phonemes and graphemes

One way of introducing a grapheme might be to show the children a few familiar words such as *'bonjour'* and *'je'*. Ask the children to listen to words as you say them and, at the same time, to look at the written words on a board or on cards. Can they work out which letter is making the 'zh' sound [ʒ]? Is it the same in each word? The children can now create a rule, e.g. 'In French the letter 'j' makes a 'zh' sound [ʒ].'

The next step might be to create a flashcard with the grapheme on it in a large font – 'j' in this example (see **Resource: Large Grapheme Card**). Simply transfer or type in the letter/s or letter string/s. When you hold up this card the children have to say the corresponding sound. It might be helpful to assign a colour to each grapheme, or each group of graphemes that all represent the same phoneme, such as 'o', 'au' and 'eau' in French. If you consistently use the same colour coding then this might help reinforce the correspondences in some children's minds, especially with digraphs and trigraphs (two or three letters making one sound) like 'au' and 'eau' in French.

Listed below are some of the colour codes we have used in French for vowel sounds which have been used on the **PowerPoint presentation: French Vowels** (see also **Spanish Phonology** and **German Phonemes**) and used for the accompanying 'sacks' activities in French. Note that the long and short vowel sounds have been conflated on the French presentation.

a/à	red
é/er/ez	green
e	pink
è/ai/ei/	brown
i	yellow
o/au/eau	orange
ou	dark blue
u	purple
oi	grey

Games linking phonemes and graphemes

When you have introduced about four sounds, various games are possible, such as putting up the cards (these could be the sound sacks – 'sacs à sons' – described below) with corresponding graphemes on the walls and asking the children to point to the correct card as you say a sound. Further suggestions for phoneme–grapheme correspondence activities are given in Chapter 3.

Creating a 'sound bank'

At this early stage it is a good idea to create a class 'sound bank'. This could be a display book, hard-backed note book or file, which contains all the sounds (phonemes) the children have met so far and some examples of words containing them. There should be a separate page for each sound. In French some of the pages might look like this:

u	j	ou	on	in
salut	bonjour	bonjour	bonjour	bien
tu	je	douze	onze	cinq
	jaune	rouge	marron	quinze

This is something that can be kept and added to and even transferred to the next year group with the children. You can easily find words for the phoneme you are focusing on by consulting the lists of Example Words by Phoneme for the three languages on the CD (**Resource: Example Words by Phoneme**).

Sound Sacks

This activity particularly supports the KS2 Framework objective:

04.3 Listen for sounds, rhyme and rhythm – compare different sounds

An alternative to a book-based sound bank is an idea which we have adapted from some French school teachers we know who teach French children to read using French phonics. This activity gets the children thinking about the sounds of the foreign language and can be introduced right from the first lesson by using 'borrowed' words such as '*croissant*' and '*gâteau*'. This also means that families can become involved and trips to the supermarket take on a whole new twist!

Place sound sacks or 'Sacs à sons' around the classroom, either as poster sheets (see **Resource: Single Phoneme Sack**) or as actual cloth bags. Each sack will have a label with the spellings of the sound. When you say a sound, the children should put objects that have the designated sound in their names in the appropriate sound sack or near the poster. They can also write or bring in words written on paper or card that have the sound in them and stick them on the appropriate poster or in the sack. Words like '*bonjour*' can be written twice and put in two different sacks: 'ou' and 'on'. (See **Resource: Words by Phoneme for Objects and Visuals**.)

There are also worksheets with sound sacks for older children to complete individually or as pairs. These are available in black and white or colour (on the CD) – see **Resource: Vowel Sacks Worksheet b&w** and **Vowel Sacks Worksheet colour** for each language. Similar sacks and worksheets can be made by consulting the **Key Phoneme Guides** at the end of the book.

New words can be added as they come up in lessons. For example, if you are doing some work on animals you could ask the children to consider the word '*tortue*' and decide which sound sacks he could live in.

Support
A simple place to start is with words the children already know. In English there are lots of words borrowed from French relating to food. For example, a child might bring in a cr**oi**ssant wrapper to put in the 'oi' [wa] sack, whereas another may contribute an empty qui**ch**e box for the 'ch' [ʃ] sack. Think of the fun you could have with an empty bag of chicken goujons deciding whether it goes into the 'ou' [u], 'j' [ʒ] or 'on' [ɔ̃] sack!

Extension
This is an open-ended activity, which means that each child can work at their own level, working with the particular phonemes and range of phonemes they feel comfortable with.

Revisiting
Once you have introduced some graphemes and are doing more work on sound-spelling links this will be a useful activity in supporting the phoneme–grapheme correspondence work discussed in Chapter 3. The objects can be

replaced with written words on cards and the children will be able to see how the same phoneme is sometimes represented by several different letter strings (graphemes), certainly in French.

Shopping Baskets

This activity is very similar to the Sound Sacks game but the children work in teams to collect sounds. Although the children will find this activity great fun, they are also likely to find it quite tricky. They are listening for phonemes within words and, although they are only listening for one particular phoneme each, the activity involves listening to a wide range of different phonemes, all within words, and sifting out the one they need.

Put the children in groups then give each group a shopping basket or alternative, such as a box or bag. (An ideal resource is a P.E. bag that has a plastic pocket on the front where a label can be inserted.) Label the basket/box/bag with a letter or letter string, in other words a grapheme, and give one to each group. This is the sound that they are trying to collect. You have a separate bag of objects. (See **Resource: Words by Phoneme for Objects and Visuals** for ideas.) One at a time you take an object out of the bag and ask who would like it, e.g. *'Qui veut un chameau?'* ('Who wants a camel?'). The children who are collecting either 'ch' [ʃ] words or 'au/eau' [o] words need to call *'moi'* or *'moi, s'il vous plaît!'* ('Me, please!'), whatever phrase you have decided on. Whoever is the first group to call out wins the object for their basket/bag. If you choose the words carefully there will always be at least two teams competing for each object, which the children love. At the end of the game the team with the most objects is the winner. You can adapt the phrases you use in the game to what you might be practising in language lessons, such as 'I would like' or 'I need'.

Support
As this is a team game, children can use peer support. Less confident children will wait for their team mates to call out but they will nevertheless be learning by listening. This works initially but there is a danger that the quickest/loudest/most confident few will take over and other children will be left out. If this happens you will need to adapt the activity. You could go around the groups, clockwise, asking each group in turn whether they need that item. The first group to say 'yes' gets the item. With the next object continue asking the groups from the point you had reached. This also avoids a lot of shouting out and excessive noise.

As with other activities, the particular phoneme the children have to listen for is important. Easily identifiable phonemes such as 'ch' [ʃ] in French are simpler for the children than some of the French nasal sounds, which are similar to each other.

To simplify the activity for everyone, just keep to about three phonemes, all of which are quite distinct from each other, such as 'ch' [ʃ], 'oi' [wa] and 'é' [e] in French.

Extension
As the children become more confident you can repeat this activity with a greater range of phonemes and include those which are very similar to each other, such as the French nasal sounds.

Phoneme Salad

This is played the same way as the well-known 'fruit salad' game. Sit the children in a circle. Choose a small number of phonemes, such as 'o' [o], 'ch' [ʃ], 'oi' [wa] and 'é' [e]. Go around the circle allocating one phoneme per child. For example, the first child gets 'o' [o], the second child gets 'ch' [ʃ], the third gets 'oi' [wa] and the fourth gets 'é' [e]. By the fifth child you are back to 'o' [o] again. This means that there will be several children listening out for each phoneme. The game begins with you calling out one phoneme, e.g. 'ch' [ʃ]. All the children who are listening for that sound must jump up and swap places while you try to 'steal' one of their places. If you succeed, the child whose place you have taken must go in the middle as the caller. You may need to support new callers by giving them two phonemes to pick from so they only have to repeat the one they want.

If you are calling out individual phonemes this activity is simpler than the Shopping Baskets activity above. If you progress to calling out words containing key phonemes then the activity practises the same skills as the Shopping Baskets activity but without peer support.

Support
Start with individual phonemes and have a small number of phonemes, e.g. four, which are easily distinguished from one another, as described above.

As mentioned above, some children may need help when it is their turn to be the caller. You can do this in a sensitive way by reminding them of the choice of phonemes, so that they only need to repeat one.

At the word-level stage, this activity provides a useful opportunity to observe the children and see who is able to identify a particular phoneme in a word and who finds that difficult. You may even be able to tell which particular phonemes are proving tricky for the children.

Extension
Progress to calling out words containing the phonemes, a greater number of different phonemes and ones which are similar to each other, such as 'in' [ɛ̃] and 'an' [ɑ̃].

Pots of Phonemes

This is a calmer, quieter activity than Phoneme Salad or Shopping Baskets. It involves the children thinking about each word, saying it aloud and then working out which individual phonemes they can hear. The activity also requires the children to know a reasonable amount of vocabulary. For that reason it is perhaps an activity that is better suited to children who are at least in their **second year** of studying the language. It would be a useful activity for revisiting key phonemes with Years 5 and 6.

This is an activity which has been adapted from a typical literacy activity. Gather some plastic pots, boxes (such as shoe boxes) or cartons (such as ice cream tubs). Fill each one with small objects that all contain a particular phoneme. For example, in French the 'ch' [ʃ] box might contain a toy cat (*chat*), dog (*chien*), horse (*cheval*), cow (*vache*), a bar of chocolate (*chocolat*) and a cork (*bouchon*). Divide the class into groups and give each a box. Each group must decide what key phoneme is in the box by working out which sound all the objects have in common. The children are allowed to ask you for help with vocabulary if they do not know the name of an item. Once they have guessed they can swap boxes with another group.

Use the resource lists (**Resources: Example Words by Phoneme; Words by Phoneme for Objects and Visuals**) for ideas of what to include in your pots. This activity involves 'sourcing' a large number of objects. The larger your boxes or pots the greater flexibility you have with the items that will fit. Ask the children to help you by bringing in an item from home (making sure that it is not valuable or fragile and that they have permission, of course). You could ask different groups of children to bring in items for a particular sound or you could have a 'phoneme of the week' and ask the whole class to bring in objects with that sound, moving on to a new phoneme the following week. You may have to help the children by discussing with them some words they know in the foreign language that contain a particular phoneme. If you have created a class 'sound bank' as described earlier in this chapter (page 17) it will be a useful source of ideas for the children.

Sounds & Words – Supporting language learning through phonics

Clapping Game

Children are used to clapping to work out the number of syllables in a word in English. You can use the same activity to practise breaking foreign language words into syllables.

Syllable Tennis

Once the children are able to clap out syllables you can introduce a 'tennis' game. This activity provides further practice in counting how many syllables there are in a word but will also start the children thinking about where the syllable divisions occur.

Pick a few examples to discuss first, e.g. in French 'a-ni-mal'. If it were 'an-i-mal' then the first syllable would be the nasal sound 'an' [ã] as in French 'grand' [gʀã]. To get started, you will need visuals on the board so the children know the words to be included such as a picture of chocolate for French 'chocolat'. (Choose words the children are already familiar with). Pretend to serve and as you mime hitting the ball call out the first syllable of a word, e.g. 'cho' [ʃɔ] in French. The children return serve and call out the next syllable 'co' [kɔ] and the game continues until one side has the last syllable – in this example 'lat' [la] (to make the word 'chocolat'). You can pretend to smash the ball to end the point.

As soon as you have illustrated the game to the whole class, get the children to play this in pairs.

Support

If children are finding this difficult, encourage them to go back to clapping out the syllables first. Select words the children already know or which will be easy for you to explain. You could support them by arranging visuals on the board in columns according to the number of syllables, e.g. under the column labelled '2' put a picture of a pig – 'cochon' for French. Under the column labelled '3' a picture of a bar of chocolate.

Example words, listed by number of syllables with recordings, are available in French, Spanish and German (see **Resource: Words by Syllable Count**).

Revisiting

This is an activity you can keep returning to. In Year 3 most children will be happy just thinking about the number of syllables. By Year 6 some will be able to consider syllable division as described above and may like to try the **Count the Syllables** worksheet activities (see **Resource: Count the Syllables Worksheet**).

Further activities on syllables are presented in Chapter 4 where activities focus on the written word.

» Support for non-language specialists

Some KS2 teachers who are not language specialists worry about their pronunciation. Obviously, it is important to provide an accurate model of pronunciation for the children. However, this does not mean that you have to be fluent or have an accent that is virtually a native speaker's pronunciation. Nevertheless, you will feel happier and more confident if you practise the words, phrases, sentences, songs and teaching activities a number of times on your own or with a colleague so that your phonics work with the children flows smoothly.

A key question we are often asked is 'In what order should we introduce the phonemes?' There are no hard and fast rules about this. One solution might be to start with the sounds you are confident of pronouncing correctly. In French these will typically include 'oi' [wa], 'é' [e], 'ch' [ʃ], 'j' [ʒ], and 'ou' [u], but 'u' [y] and the nasal sounds, 'un' [œ̃], 'on' [ɔ̃], 'in' [ɛ̃], 'an' [ã], can be tricky.

Some teachers prefer to introduce the sounds as they occur. Research has shown, though, that just as when teaching English phonics, the most effective approach is to be as explicit and systematic as possible.

Nevertheless, as the children meet new words and practise saying them it is a good opportunity to focus on some of the individual sounds that make up those words. For example, in the first few French lessons you will probably introduce 'bonjour' and 'salut'. From these words you might choose to focus on the sound 'on' [ɔ̃], 'u' [y] or 'j' [ʒ], leading children to find these sounds in other words. Of course, it is always a good idea to revisit sounds already covered.

Sometimes a song or rhyme will have a particular sound repeated, presenting an ideal opportunity for practising that sound with the children (and/or yourself!), such as the phoneme 'en/an' [ɑ̃] in the Christmas carol 'Vive le vent' (see 'Phoneme Towers', page 15).

If there are sounds that you want to practise with the children but which you are not confident of pronouncing correctly yourself, you will need some support. If you know of a native speaker (perhaps a parent) who can help, then ask them to work with you on making the sounds. You could contact your local secondary school and a member of the languages department may be able to help you. They might even have a foreign language assistant (FLA) who could help. Try to get an actual demonstration of how to make the sound with your mouth and lips, then practise these new moves. You can even create pseudo-words using the new sound/s. In French, for instance, practise moving your lips and mouth to say rapidly:

- si .... (big smile)
- sa ....(dropped jaw)
- so .... (fully rounded, protruding lips)
- su .... (rounded but pinched lips, upper lip somewhat drawn down over the upper teeth)
- sé .... (with a half-smile, like saying the letter 'a' in English but with no diphthong 'ay-ee' sound).

Then try these vowels with different beginning consonants, for instance, 'm', 'l', 't', etc.

The **PowerPoint** presentations in French, Spanish and German show you how to make these and other key sounds. You can also refer to the **Key Phoneme Guides** at the end of the book and the recordings (**Recording: Individual Phonemes**) for all three languages.

> **By the end of this chapter** most children should be able to identify several common phonemes in the language they are studying, including some that do not occur in English. They should also be able to pronounce several of the phonemes with reasonable accuracy.
>
> Some children will be able to identify a smaller number of phonemes and may need support such as emphasis and repetition. When pronouncing phonemes that do not occur in English they may need to repeat the sound after a model, such as the teacher, or a recording.
>
> Other children will be able to identify a large range of phonemes and be able to listen for more than one sound at a time in a spoken text. Some may be able to pronounce most of the common phonemes accurately and have started to understand how they are represented in written form.

Chapter 2
» Distinguishing between phonemes

Topics covered in this chapter

Activities for distinguishing between phonemes

In this chapter we provide further emphasis on distinguishing foreign language phonemes from each other when they are spoken or heard. We stated earlier that very early on human beings form sound categories in their brains, based on their earliest language/s experience, even before birth. It can take a lot of paying attention and practising to develop new sound categories for the new language and it is easy to slide two similar sounds together in your memory. The ultimate effect is that you are not sure about the word you are hearing or about how to pronounce it. Later on, when dealing with the written word spelling may become a problem. In addition, you will not be able to decode it easily when reading, or to understand the meaning of the written word when understanding depends on your decoding it correctly.

Once children have been introduced to several key phonemes and have practised listening for them and saying them, it is helpful, as pointed out in Chapter 1 to introduce some activities to help them **distinguish** one phoneme from another very similar phoneme such as 'ou' [u] and 'u' [y] in French. There are lots of sorting activities that can be done and you can also adapt activities from KS1 literacy. If you do not teach KS1 literacy yourself, try to observe a colleague or to discuss his/her preferred literacy activities for phoneme differentiation with the children. These can then be used for the foreign language, often to the children's delighted recognition.

» KS2 Framework links

All the activities in this chapter are linked to the KS2 Framework objective for Year 4:

O4.3 Listen for sounds, rhyme and rhythm – compare different sounds

As we frequently point out in this book, the activities can be used with any year group with some appropriate adaptation.

» Activities for distinguishing between phonemes

The following activities include those we have found to be useful and often good fun.

They are all based on careful listening and remembering.

Sounds & Words – Supporting language learning through phonics

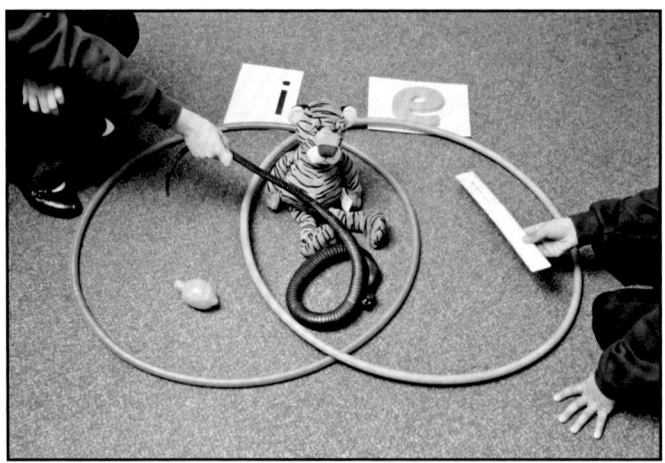

Physical Phoneme Venn Diagrams

This activity helps children to identify individual phonemes in words and to distinguish one phoneme from another, similar, phoneme. You may notice that it also links to maths work in Years 3 and 4. You might like to use this activity if you have noticed that the children are confusing two sounds. When the children are playing this in pairs it also presents a useful opportunity for assessment, especially where you have previously noticed some confusion. Children can monitor, and help, each other. (See **Resource: Words for Phoneme Distinguishing**.)

Place two large hoops on the floor overlapping them so they represent a Venn diagram (see below). Label each hoop with a letter or letter string corresponding to two key phonemes you have been practising, e.g. 'oi' [wa] and 'eau' [o] in French or 'i' [i] and 'e' [e] in Spanish. Ask for about six volunteers and get them to stand at the front and give each an object or a picture card to hold. The words for the objects should contain one or both of the key phonemes to be practised. In turn, each volunteer holds up their object and, with your help, says what it is. The rest of the class decides which hoop it belongs in. If the word contains both sounds then the object is placed in the centre section where the hoops overlap. To finish off, have the children say the names of the objects. Check that they are pronouncing the sounds correctly – distinguishing between the phonemes orally.

The children can continue this game in pairs with a couple of hoops per pair and a set of objects for them to sort. The playground or hall would be ideal for this activity but it could be adapted for work in the classroom, using small circles, or pictures of circles on paper (see **Resource: Venn Diagram** or you can draw your own).

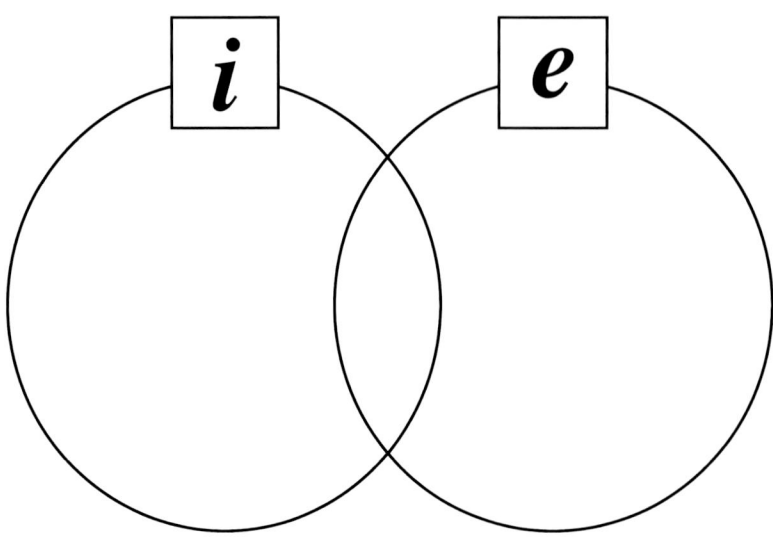

Sounds & Words – Supporting language learning through phonics

Possible words in Spanish for objects or pictures, which the teacher should say slowly and clearly, could include, for example:

i	e	i + e
limón	tren	serpiente
boli	té	tigre
piña	regla	
lapiz	coche	

Example objects for a Venn Diagram with French 'oi' [wa] and 'au'/'eau' [o].

Example objects for a Venn Diagram with German long 'e' [eː] and short 'a' [a].

For words in all three languages including objects likely to be found in the classroom, see **Recording** and **Resource: Words for Phoneme Distinguishing** and **Recording: Words for Sorting Exercises**.

Distinguishing between phonemes

Support

If children find this activity difficult, go back to the type of activities detailed in Chapter 1 and encourage them to listen for just one sound to begin with. Using just one hoop, they can decide whether an object belongs in the hoop or not. Once each sound has been practised individually, the children can progress to distinguishing between them. Working in pairs offers the opportunity for peer support.

Extension

Some children might be ready to progress to thinking of their own, additional objects to include in one of the hoops. Some might even enjoy the challenge of creating their own hoop activity for others to complete, using two new sounds and a new set of objects (or picture cards). See **Resource: Words by Phoneme for Objects and Visuals**.

Phoneme Islands

This is another sorting activity that practises the same phoneme identification skills as the previous activity. It can be played on the interactive whiteboard using pictures for the children to drag and drop. Alternatively you can use a normal whiteboard, or flipchart paper and picture cards that the children stick on. There will not necessarily be any connection between the items of vocabulary other than the sounds they contain and the children do not need to know the words already – it will help them focus purely on the sounds they hear rather than be thinking of the spellings.

Draw a simple outline of two islands (see below) and label each with a different phoneme – the two sounds you want the children to practise differentiating.

Spread out the pictures on a table or stick them randomly on a blank area of wall. The pictures should all be of words containing one of the two phonemes being practised. Invite a volunteer to select a picture and show it to the class. You say the word slowly and clearly several times and the class decides on which island the item belongs. For example, *'poule'* goes on 'ou' island and *'tortue'* goes on 'u' island. The volunteer sticks the picture on the correct island and then a different volunteer takes over.

ou	u
(la) poule (hen)	(la) jupe (skirt)
(le) genou (knee)	(la) tortue (tortoise)
(la) bouche (mouth)	(la) lune (moon)
(le) mouton (sheep)	(du) sucre (sugar)
(le) loup (wolf)	(le) pull (sweater)

For further suggestions for words, refer to **Recording: Words for Phoneme Distinguishing** and **Resource: Words for Phoneme Distinguishing**.

Note: In French, using the indirect article ('*un*'/'*une*') for this particular activity can be confusing as '*une*' contains one of the key phonemes itself: '*une poule*'. You may prefer to use an article at all times to reinforce gender, in which case use the **definite** article ('*le*'/'*la*') as above.

Support

You can do this activity with just one phoneme and one island. In this version, have some pictures of items that clearly don't contain the sound (they will not get on to the island!). This effectively turns it into one of the phoneme-identifying activities similar to those in Chapter 1.

u	not u
(la) jupe (skirt)	(le) singe (monkey)
(la) tortue (tortoise)	(la) porte (door)
(la) lune (moon)	(le) bateau (boat)
(du) sucre (sugar)	(la) règle (ruler)
(le) pull (sweater)	(le) chat (cat)

Extension

The activity can be made more challenging by choosing two phonemes that are particularly similar, e.g. the French nasal sounds 'in' [ɛ̃] and 'an' [ɑ̃] or long and short vowels in German.

The children can also be encouraged to create their own suggestions for items, perhaps using the sound banks described in Chapter 1 (page 17). If the children are keen and ready, there is no reason not to begin the pronunciation of the sounds, showing the children how to make the sounds with their mouths, tongues and lips (refer to the **Key Phoneme Guides** at the end of the book and **Recording: Individual Phonemes,** and the **PowerPoint** presentations).

Odd One Out

This is a very simple activity that can be used as a quick check or practice activity if, during a lesson, you become aware of the children confusing two sounds, for example 'ou' and 'u' in French.

If you are not confident producing the sounds yourself then use the recorded sound files (**Recording: Distinguishing Phonemes – Odd One Out**) or ask a colleague from the languages department at your local secondary school to help.

Tell the children to listen very carefully as you say five sounds and to decide which is the odd one out. Then you say, for example, 'ou [u] ... u [y] ... ou ... ou ... ou'. It helps if you hold up a finger each time you say a sound. Ask the children which sound was different. In our example it was the second sound so the children should say '*deux*' or hold up two fingers. (For other examples, see **Resource: Distinguishing Phonemes – Odd One Out**.)

Support
This activity can be used as a support in itself, either with the whole class, a group or an individual child as and when you feel they are struggling to hear the difference between two similar sounds. You may need to repeat

it several times and, if they are still finding it difficult, slow down and really exaggerate the sounds. If the children have difficulty with your saying five sounds, try four or three.

Extension
In the same way that the activity can be simplified by slowing down and exaggerating the sounds, the reverse is true. As children become more confident and skilled in differentiating sounds you can speed up the delivery. This can become a game where you try to catch the children out and they will love the challenge.

Running Game

This simple activity, which is still based on the sorting principle but is more kinaesthetic and, perhaps, more memorable, is a running game between two points – like the running game 'Same as English or Different?' (page 12). It can be played in the hall or outside, running between two walls, two posts or two cones. Designate one wall as the first phoneme (e.g. 'ou') and the other wall as the second phoneme (e.g. 'u'). The children stand in between the two walls (or posts) and listen as you call out a phoneme (see **Recording: Sorting Phonemes** and **Resource: Sorting Phonemes**). They must then run to the appropriate wall. After each go the children should return to the centre so they are close to you to hear each sound clearly. This can be played as an elimination game, with the children becoming 'out' if they run the wrong way – although it is worth keeping a careful eye on children in this sort of game as it sometimes throws up children who have hearing problems.

Support
Children tend to find it easier to distinguish between two phonemes when that is all they have to listen for, i.e. not for the sound **within** a word.

Extension
Listening for phonemes within words tends to be trickier, so a progression would be to move on to calling out words containing one of the phonemes being practised, e.g. '*poule*' or '*tortue*'. See **Recording: Words for Sorting Exercises**.

> **By the end of this chapter** most children should be able to hear the difference between two similar-sounding phonemes in the foreign language. Some children will need to hear the phonemes on their own, spoken very slowly and clearly. Other children may be able to hear the difference between similar phonemes when heard in whole words.
>
> This chapter has emphasised the learner being able to distinguish phonemes when they are heard.

Chapter 3
» Phoneme–grapheme correspondence

Topics covered in this chapter

When to introduce the written word

Confusion with English

Activities for focusing on differences between sound-spelling links

In this chapter we focus on how the sounds which the children have learned to hear and produce are represented in their written form. We start with some general observations about timing the introduction of the written forms. We look at how to deal with possible confusions with English spellings of sounds. There are then a series of activities for reinforcing the learner's explicit link between the sound and its spelling/s, first at single phoneme level, then in simple syllables.

It is best to introduce a limited number of phonemes and their spellings at a time, for instance using the PowerPoint presentations that accompany this book.

» When to introduce the written word

One of the most frequently asked questions by teachers of languages is when to introduce the written word. Often language specialists advise against introducing it too early or else the children will tend to 'say what they see'. This becomes evident in their pronunciation and is especially obvious in French with examples such as 'lappin' (pronounced to rhyme with the English word pin) for *'lapin'* and 'sty-low' for *'stylo'*. However, introducing the written word too late can also have its drawbacks. Often the children will be imagining the words in their head as they hear them and some even write them down, using their own phonetic system. It is then a real shock when they do eventually see the written words. 'Oiseau' is always a surprise, starting with 'oi' instead of the 'wa' they have been envisaging. Similarly *'poisson'* is envisaged as 'pwasson'.

The reason for these errors is that the children are applying the English phonetic system to French words. If they have never been taught the foreign language sound-spelling system they have no other choice than to use English, all the way to GCSE in some cases!

So, if there are inherent dangers in introducing the written word too early and too late, what is the answer? We believe it is important to introduce the written word to children early on in their language learning. The important thing is to make the sound-spelling links (the phoneme–grapheme correspondences) explicit, systematic and as complete as possible. This way the children will start to see patterns between words and will not have to rely on English phonics. In addition, they will see that other sound-spelling systems, for instance, in French and especially in Spanish and German, are far more consistent, or transparent than in English. Once they know that the sound 'wa' [wa] in French is written 'oi' the word *'oiseau'* no longer looks so shocking. They will even be able to work out some basic phonetic rules. For example, once they hear and see the words *'chat'*, *'chien'*, *'cheval'* and *'cochon'* the children should be able to work out the rule that 'in French the letters 'ch' are pronounced like 'sh' [ʃ], or 'the sound 'shh' [ʃ] is written as 'ch' in French.' The key is for you as the teacher to help the children become aware of the phoneme–grapheme rules and be able to apply them consistently.

Sounds & Words – Supporting language learning through phonics

Acquiring the basic rules of the sound-spelling system of a language can be very empowering for language learners. Patterns start to emerge, things start to make a little more sense and words are no longer just a series of random letters, the order of which must be memorised in order to write anything down. Children are also able to apply these rules to help them pronounce new words and being asked to read something aloud is no longer such a terrifying task. Research has shown that some children improve their decoding in English after they have learned how to decode successfully in a more 'transparent' language like Spanish, German or even French.

» KS2 Framework links

The activities in this chapter and in Chapter 4 help children to develop their phoneme–grapheme skills and are linked to the following objectives of the KS2 Framework for Languages:

L3.1   **Recognise some familiar words in written form**

L3.2   **Make links between some phonemes, rhymes and spellings, and read aloud familiar words**

L4.3   **Read some familiar words and phrases aloud and pronounce them accurately**

L4.3 KAL **Use phonic (…) knowledge to support accurate pronunciation**

L4.4   **Write simple words and phrases using a model and some words from memory**

L4.4 KAL **Apply phonic (…) knowledge to write simple words and phrases**

» Confusion with English

As discussed in the Introduction, it is sometimes a concern for teachers, especially of Year 3, that children might start to confuse the English and foreign language phonetic systems. However, simply avoiding talking about the phonetic system in the foreign language is not the best solution. Instead, try to make the differences explicit, comparing and contrasting. Rather than putting each language in a separate 'box', refer to the foreign language, when relevant, during Literacy work and refer to English when studying the foreign language. Sometimes you will find that the foreign language work supports work in English. For example, knowing that 'ch' is pronounced differently in French helps to explain why the word 'chef' is pronounced as it is. Later on, when you start to look at derivations of English words with the class, you will find that knowledge of the sound-spelling system of a language such as French, Spanish or German proves really useful.

» Activities for focusing on differences between sound-spelling links

Below is an activity which helps children focus on the differences between the sound-spelling links in two different languages (and have great fun doing so!).

Arguing Football Stars

This activity is linked to the KS2 Framework objective for Year 3:

O3.2 Recognise and respond to sound patterns and words – Identify phonemes which are the same as or different from English and other known languages.

This activity provides practice in pronouncing key phonemes but its main purpose is to compare and contrast phoneme–grapheme correspondences in English with those of the foreign language, making differences more explicit and thus reducing possible confusion.

Get two confident volunteers to take on the role of a famous French person and a famous English person. These might be a couple of footballers such as Thierry Henri and Steven Gerrard. They can then have a playful argument about a particular letter string, such as 'ch', with 'Gerrard' shouting the usual English sound [tʃ] (as in 'cheese') and 'Henri' disagreeing and making a 'sh' sound [ʃ]. The children can be encouraged to act the part, adding to the dialogue e.g. *'non, non, non'*. You can even print out photos and create a mask of each personality for the children to wear. Once this has been demonstrated by the volunteers the rest of the class can try it out in pairs. You may need to do some research on the internet or amongst the children in order to choose contemporary French, Spanish and German football stars they know.

Support

You may wish to divide the class in half with each half taking on the role of one of the footballers. In this way less secure children can practise the sound in chorus before they are asked to work in pairs or volunteers are asked to demonstrate.

Extension

As the children increase their knowledge of phoneme–grapheme correspondences in the foreign language they might like to suggest another grapheme that could be used in this activity. You can give a group or pair a mini card and they can act out the argument orally before the rest of the class is challenged to say what the spelling or grapheme is.

See **Resource: Mini Grapheme Cards.**

Phoneme–Grapheme Running Game

This activity is linked to the KS2 Framework objective for Year 3:

L3.2 Make links between some phonemes, rhymes and spellings, and read aloud familiar words – Pronounce accurately the most commonly used characters, letters and letter strings. Read aloud a familiar sentence, rhyme or poem.

This is a useful activity for increasing children's knowledge of phoneme–grapheme correspondence, in other words, matching sounds to letters and groups of letters. The ability to do this will really help the children pronounce new words when they see them and to spell words by thinking of the sounds they contain. Doing this sort of activity early in the children's language-learning (in the first half of Year 3) will avoid them getting a shock when they see familiar words written down for the first time. As mentioned at the beginning of this chapter, if children have been taught that the letter string 'oi' makes the sound 'wa', they won't expect *'oiseau'* to start with 'wa' and *'poisson'* to begin 'pwa' as can happen. In German the two digraphs 'ei' and 'ie' often pose difficulties for learners because they get confused with English. This is partly, we suspect, because these two spellings have so many different possible pronunciations in English. In German the phonemes are **always** the same for these two spellings: 'ei' = [aɪ] and 'ie' = [iː]. This running game activity – ideal for a P.E. warm-up in the hall, also adapted for whiteboard or tabletop use as described in Chapter 2 (page 30) – is a good opportunity to practise identifying the 'ie' and 'ei' spellings in German.

Place large text cards of letters and letter strings on the walls around the hall (see **Resource: Large Grapheme Card**). The letters should correspond to key phonemes you have been practising. The children jog around the hall and, when you call out a sound, they run to the corresponding card. This can be played as an elimination game if you wish. If the children become so good that you can't get them out (and they will!) you could have the rule that the last few to arrive are eliminated.

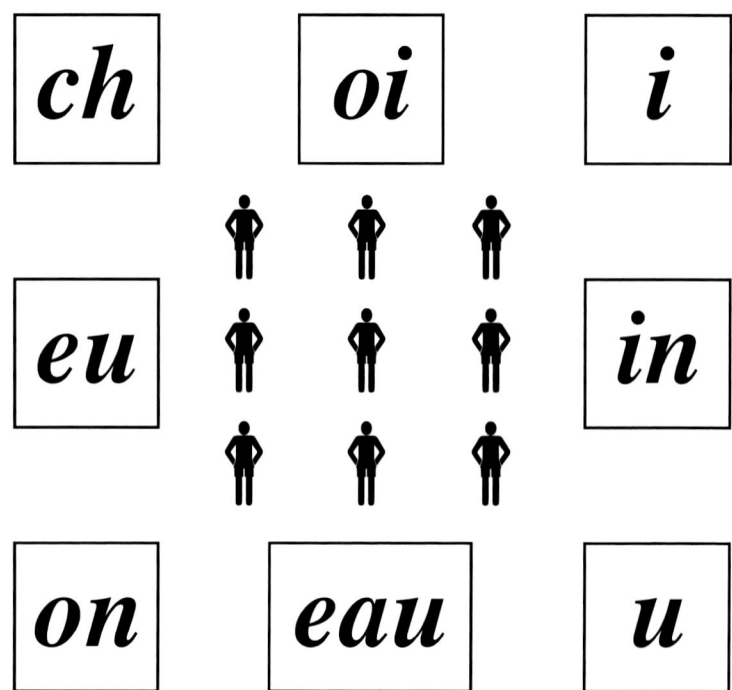

You can progress from calling out sounds to calling out words containing those sounds. The words may contain more than one key phoneme (e.g. '*oiseau*' contains the phonemes 'oi' [wa] and 'eau' [o]; '*cochon*' contains the phonemes 'ch' [ʃ] and 'on' [õ]). This makes the game even more exciting as the children will have a choice of cards and can later be challenged to run to the sound cards in the order that the phonemes occur in the word.

Support
Start small, perhaps with just four sounds – or even two as described in Chapter 2 – on cards. It is easier if these sounds are all very different, such as 'ch', 'oi', 'é' and 'j'. If you find some sounds difficult to pronounce yourself (the French nasal sounds can be tricky) then this is a good way to start. Start with sounds you are comfortable producing and gradually build up your repertoire. Use the recordings to practise and to check your pronunciation.

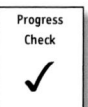

Children who find this activity difficult will rely on peer support, tending to follow the other children. It is useful to observe the children carefully to see who is confident and who needs to follow others. Do not discourage this 'following' as the children will still be learning by watching which card their friends move to when they hear certain sounds. Your observation, however, might highlight the need for some further work on particular sounds with certain children and then sound-spelling links.

Extension
Eventually you could invite some of the more confident children to take over your role as caller. They could use their memory of words they have learned or use a card containing a list of words, or a selection of word cards. The list can be provided by you or compiled by them using a word bank or picture dictionary or the lists of **Example Words by Phoneme** (**Resource**) – you do not need to include the genders or translations (they are to support your knowledge). Children learning French could propose and possibly make new cards with other spellings that have been introduced for a particular phoneme, e.g. [o].

In German, with older children, long and short vowel sounds could be practised with this game as an important first step to spelling and writing in German. Devise with the children a symbol for a long vowel like the [oː] as in 'Rose', and a symbol for a short vowel like the [ɔ] as in 'Sonne'. These could be random symbols like a dash and a triangle, as suggested on page 6 of *The literacy link* (CILT, 2001) instead of using letters. After playing the game with long and short vowel sounds by themselves, use the German list of **Example Words by Phoneme** (**Resource**) and include words the children have not learned yet.

Phoneme Families

This activity is an alternative to the phoneme–grapheme running game but it also gives the children plenty of opportunity to practise **producing** the key phonemes. You can use it to check their pronunciation if you wish.

Create a set of cards, enough for one per child, each card bearing one of about five graphemes (letters or letter strings relating to key phonemes) such as 'oi', 'u', 'é', 'j' and 'ch' in French. Hand out the cards, one to each child and tell them to keep their card secret. At your signal the children must circulate around the room, repeatedly making the sound on their card, e.g. 'oi, oi, oi, oi, oi' [wa] in French. They must try to find others with the same sound and form a group or 'family'. This activity has the potential to be lots of fun as the children move around the classroom making sounds.

See **Resource: Mini Grapheme Cards** for cards that you can change and simply put in the graphemes you wish to practise. The cards will need to be cut up before use.

Support
The first time you do this activity you might like to keep it very simple and only have four different phonemes (and, therefore, just four 'families'). This increases the likelihood of children hearing the same sound and will provide support for those unsure of their pronunciation.

Extension
You can differentiate this activity by carefully selecting which cards you give certain children. For example, in French, challenge some children with the tricky 'u' sound whilst others will be more comfortable with 'ou' [u] or 'j' [ʒ]. More confident children can be further challenged with alternative spellings of key phonemes, e.g. 'eau' rather than 'o'.

Similarly, in German an extension would be to use sounds that are more difficult to produce like 'z' [ts], 'pf' [pf], or 'zw' [tsv].

Revisiting
This is an activity you can return to, increasing the number of different graphemes as the children build up their repertoire and increase in confidence. This can also be used later to practise **final silent consonants** after vowel phonemes in French: '-ot', '-ots', '-eaux' when these spellings appear on cards for the phoneme [o]. See the Silent letters section in Chapter 4 (page 47) and the **Key Phoneme Guide** for French (page 67).

Phoneme–Grapheme Lotto

Give the children, individually or in pairs, a laminated lotto card with six letters/letter strings representing the key sounds you have been practising, e.g.

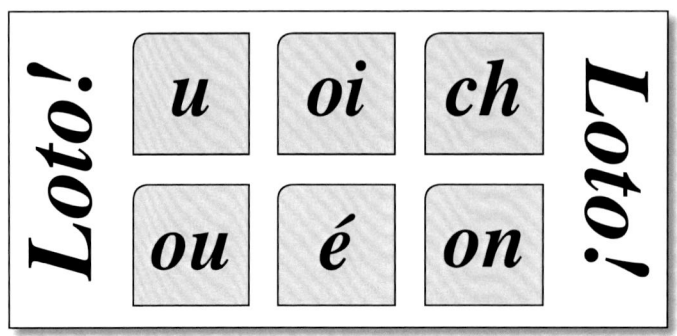

Call out a sound and each child with the corresponding grapheme crosses it off. For a simple, no-preparation variation, get the children to create their own using mini whiteboards. Alternatively, use the set of 24 lotto cards (see **Resource: Lotto Cards**), which can be used as a template for other combinations.

Support
Working in pairs will provide support for those less confident with this task and the lotto cards can be differentiated so that some cards have 'trickier' graphemes such as the nasal sounds in French, final silent letters or 'ie' and 'ei' in German.

Extension
As with the phoneme–grapheme running game, you can progress to calling out **words** containing the key phonemes, making the activity more challenging as the children have to identify several phonemes in the word.

If you already have picture lotto cards for practising vocabulary, you could re-use them for this task, e.g. the children might have animal lotto cards with six pictures of different animals.

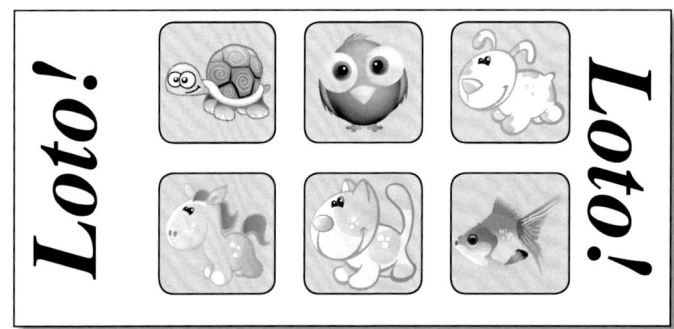

Call out a phoneme such as [wa] ('oi' in French) and anyone with an animal containing that sound can cross it off. In this example the child would be able to cross off the bird '**oi**seau' and the fish 'p**oi**sson'. See **Resource: Words by Phoneme for Objects and Visuals**.

Phonic Fans

Create, or get the children to create, some fans just like number fans but with key graphemes rather than numbers. To save time you could use existing number fans and simply adapt them by putting the graphemes over the numbers on sticky labels (or use **Resource: Phonic Fan** if preferred).

Call out a phoneme and the child identifies it on the fan by holding up the correct grapheme. This can be played initially as a team game. The children work in teams and win points for being the first team to hold up the correct grapheme when you call out a sound. You can then use the fans as a practice activity or assessment tool to check the children's knowledge of phoneme–grapheme correspondence.

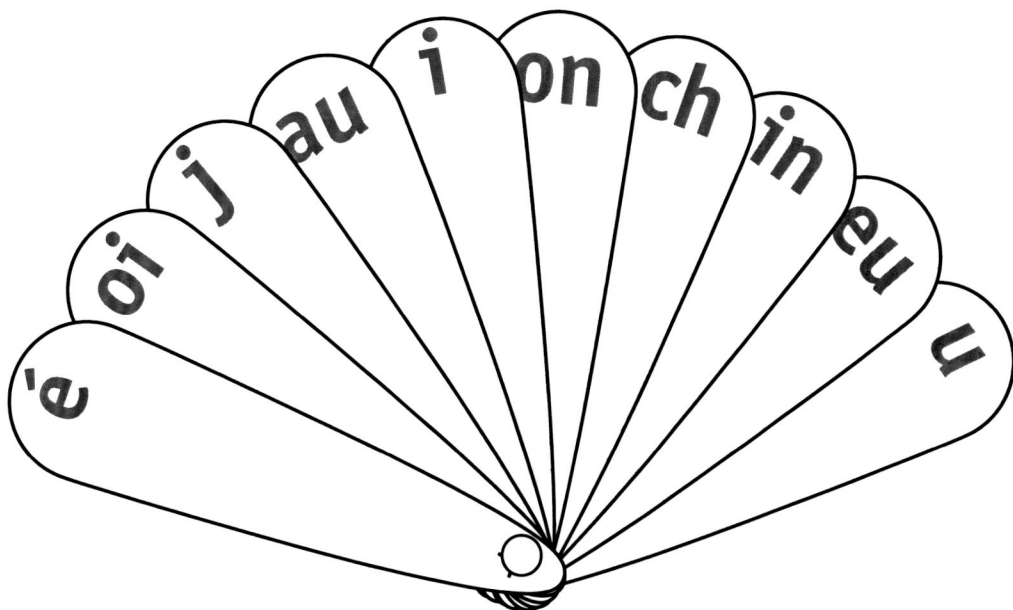

Support

The fans can be simplified by only including five graphemes initially so that half the panels are blank. This obviously reduces the number of different sounds the children need to listen for and match.

This also works well if you have the graphemes on individual cards rather than joined together as a fan. Each team has a set of cards with key graphemes on them (see **Resource: Mini Grapheme Cards**). The children can share the cards out so that each team member is responsible for just one or a couple of cards. This takes away some of the pressure as each child only has to listen out for one or two sounds and has the chance to choose cards that he or she knows.

If you have time for a second game, or next time you play, the children can be encouraged to swap cards so that they are listening for different sounds.

Extension

As the children become more proficient at matching sounds to letters and letter strings you can increase the number of different graphemes and/or include some more challenging ones such as the French nasal sounds. You can also use **Resource: Mini Word Cards** to put simple words that have the selected phonemes, one word per card, instead of just the grapheme. This way the learners look carefully to detect the sound said by you.

Grapheme Dice

Create your own grapheme die in under five minutes. Use a large foam die, preferably one with plastic pockets with card inserts. Write a letter/letter string on each card and place each one on each face of the die. (If your die doesn't have plastic pockets simply stick pieces of paper or card onto each face using double-sided sticky tape.) Once it is finished you can use the die for all sorts of activities.

The children line up in two teams facing each other. Throw the die into the centre and child number 1 from each team must call out the sound represented by the letters on the die, e.g. 'oi' in French. Whoever is first to call out the correct phoneme gets to sit down. Roll the die again and this time the number 2 children from each team go head to head. When everyone has had a go the team with the fewest people left standing is the winner.

A variation on this game is to ask the two children going head to head to predict the sound that will be rolled. If they are right they get a team point.

If you have several dice the children can play this game in small groups, thereby getting more turns and being more actively involved, as well as monitoring each other.

Support
As with most of these activities, keep it simple by choosing six phonemes that are easily distinguished from each other and ones with which the children are very familiar.

Extension
You can progress to more challenging sets of graphemes and phonemes such as, in French, the nasal sounds 'un' [œ̃], 'on' [ɔ̃], 'in' [ɛ̃], 'an' [ɑ̃], with a couple of alternative spellings (different graphemes) such as 'en' [ɑ̃] and 'ein' [ɛ̃]. Final vowel sounds that are followed by silent consonants could also be used, e.g. '-at', '-ots' or '-eux'.

Match-up

Use recordings of individual sounds (**Recording: Individual Phonemes**) to give the children practice in matching sounds to their corresponding letter(s), in other words matching phonemes to graphemes. This can be a simple whole-class activity on the interactive whiteboard. Arrange up to five sound files on the screen, numbering each icon. Next, add text boxes, each containing a letter or letter string but make sure they are jumbled up. The children can click on a sound and then click and drag the appropriate text box to match them up. See the **PowerPoint presentation: Match-up** for an example in French of how this might be done..

For group work, use recording devices such as 'Talking Tin Lids' (see: www.talkingproducts.co.uk). Their yellow 10-second 'lids' are ideal for recording single sounds. The lids can be mounted on card holders and the children must then listen to a sound, find the corresponding grapheme card and place it in the cardholder.

The lids can also be used to create an interactive wall display using cards (see **Resource: Mini Grapheme Cards)**, lids and long pieces of string attached by drawing pins. The children must press the button on a lid to hear the sound and then match it to the correct letter card by moving the string.

Support
If the activity is organised as pairwork the children will have some peer support. To begin with, just include a few sounds, perhaps four, and choose ones which are very distinct such as 'ch', 'ou', 'é', 'oi' in French.

Extension
The activity can be made more challenging by adding more sounds and including similar or confusing sounds, e.g. in French:

ou [u], u [y]............(hard to distinguish)
é [e].....................(children tend to associate the sound with letter 'a' because of the letter name in English)
i [i].......................(often confused with letter 'e' because of the letter name in English)
a [a] ....(letter often confused with the sound for 'é')

Extension should include other spellings for the same sound, also vowel sounds at the ends of words in French where the final consonant/s are silent (see the Silent Letters section of the **Key Phoneme Guide** for French (page 67).

Grapheme Hop

This is a further activity that helps children practise linking letters to the sounds they make (linking graphemes to phonemes). It will particularly appeal to learners who enjoy kinaesthetic activities and it is great fun – ideal for the last week of term.

The best resource to use would be large interlocking foam squares (sometimes these come with numbers on to create a hopscotch game). Re-label each square with a letter/letter string on paper.

If you don't have access to foam squares you can use sheets of A4 card or paper.

Arrange the squares in a 3x3 grid. If you are using card or paper, use sticky tape to fix the sheets to the floor to prevent the children skidding.

The children line up facing the grid. The first child calls out a sound and hops onto the appropriate square and then off onto the floor. The next child must repeat the first sound and add one, hopping onto the first square, then the new square and then off the mat. This continues until the sequence is too long to remember and the whole process starts again. The children will see it as a memory game and will focus on remembering the correct sequence without realising how much repetition is involved.

This activity is best played in small groups to maximise active involvement by the children. If space is a problem you can create your own table-top version using paper and counters or fingers.

Support
As with most of these activities, start with easier sound/spelling links and add more difficult ones as the children become more confident. You can also reduce the number of squares if the children find it too difficult.

Extension
As with the Grapheme Dice activity, you can extend the activity by including letter strings with silent letters at the end and letters with accents or umlauts. Instead of individual phonemes, children can say a word and then hop through its graphemes to spell it.

Phoneme Dictation

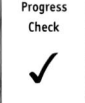

This is a simple activity that can be used to check children's progress in understanding the phoneme–grapheme correspondences of the language they are learning.

If you are not confident producing the sounds yourself then use the recorded sound files (**Recording: Individual Phonemes** or, for a sequence of phonemes, **Recording: Random Phonemes**).

Read out a series of phonemes, slowly and clearly. The children write down the corresponding letter/s on paper or a mini whiteboard. See **Resource: Random Phonemes**.

Support

As this is a progress check, you can expect the children to be at different levels. It is an exercise you can revisit from time to time, increasing the number of phonemes each time, as you have covered more. The children can record their progress using the colouring-in sheet at the end of the Can-Do statements (see **Resource: Learner's Can-Do Statements**), which includes the French key phonemes and can be adapted for other languages.

As with most of the activities, this exercise can be simplified by reducing the number of phonemes or by slowing the pace of delivery, adding pauses and repetition.

Extension

In the same way that the activity can be simplified by slowing down and exaggerating the sounds, the reverse is true. As children become more confident you can speed up the delivery. You can also increase the number of phonemes as the children have covered them. As well as using this activity as a progress check you could also turn it into an individual or team challenge. Give the children a mini whiteboard each, say a phoneme and award a point to the first person to hold up a whiteboard with the correct grapheme on it. A potentially exciting but completely silent activity!

Silly Syllables

This activity provides an intermediate step between reading graphemes for single sounds and reading whole words.

Display a set of individual syllables on the board. Together with the whole class practise reading the syllables out loud, saying them slowly and clearly. (For recordings go to **Recording: Recognising Syllables**.) After you have read them several times with the class ask smaller groups and then individuals to read them aloud.

Support

Start with adding onset consonant sounds that are the same as or very similar to English and which have phoneme–grapheme correspondences the same as English. In Spanish, for example, you could start with 'ma [ma], mo [mo], mu [mu]'. This will build the children's confidence.

Extension

You can progress to syllables containing one phoneme that is very different from English, such as 'ja [xa], jo [xo], ju [xu]' in Spanish and then introduce syllables with two phonemes that are both different from English, such as 'ge' [xe].

> **By the end of this chapter** most children should be able to match most of the main phonemes to the corresponding letter or letter string (grapheme). Some children may be able to suggest all the possible graphemes for a given sound (such as 'é', 'er' and 'ez'). A few children may also be able to match more difficult and similar-sounding phonemes (such as the French nasals) to their graphemes.
>
> Whilst we have looked explicitly at single phonemes and their spellings, some children may be able very quickly to develop whole-word reading skills, having memorised the shape of the word. This is fine. However, they also need to be able to break down the word into single phonemes as well. This supports all their other language skills, including speaking and spelling. Once you are assured a child can distinguish the individual phonemes by their spellings, proceeding on to whole-word decoding will be very easy for both you and your learners. We look at this in the next chapter.

Sounds & Words – Supporting language learning through phonics

Chapter 4
» Decoding and synthesising

Topics covered in this chapter

Decoding
Activities for decoding words
Pronouncing unfamiliar written words
Silent final letters in French
Rhyming activities
Activities for synthesising words

In this chapter we begin with a series of activities for decoding, from counting phonemes to reading syllables, words and then sentences. Following that are activities for synthesising, or writing in the foreign language. Again we begin with activities at pre-word level, working toward dictations that may involve several sentences. Decoding and synthesising are not actually developed independently of each other. You will want to pick activities for developing both skills as appropriate for the children.

Once the children are familiar with the sound-spelling links (the phoneme–grapheme correspondence) of the language, they can use this skill to help them decode words when reading and synthesise words in their writing. We include a section on silent letters, particularly important in French, and provide Support Sheets for the sounds and spellings of each language (**Resource: Sounds and Spellings Support Sheet**) for both you and the learners to use as a quick reference source for decoding and synthesising.

» KS2 Framework links

The activities in this chapter help children to develop their decoding and synthesising skills and are linked to the following objectives of the KS2 Framework for Languages:

L4.1 KAL   Apply phonic (…) knowledge of the foreign language in order to decode text

L4.2   Follow a short text, listening and reading at the same time

L4.3   Read some familiar words and phrases aloud and pronounce them accurately

L4.3 KAL   Use phonic (…) knowledge to support accurate pronunciation

L4.4   Write simple words and phrases using a model and some words from memory

L4.4 KAL   Apply phonic (…) knowledge to write simple words and phrases

L5.3 KAL   Apply phonic (…) knowledge of the new language in order to locate words in a reference source

L6.3   Match sound to sentences and paragraphs

L6.3 LLS   Apply prior knowledge of sound/spelling system to recognise the written word.

Sounds & Words – Supporting language learning through phonics

» Decoding

Decoding involves breaking down a word into its individual phonemes. If the children can do this they can read aloud many phonetically regular words, even if the words are unfamiliar to them. When introducing vocabulary it is occasionally worth showing the children a new word in written form first and asking them to work out how it is pronounced. Choose a simple one first such as *'moi'* or *'ton'*, moving on to longer words such as *'sapin'* or *'avion'* or even *'pourquoi'* all of which can be worked out in a straightforward way if the sound-spelling rules are applied. (There are many young people who reach GCSE level and are still unable to read aloud unfamiliar words. This causes embarrassment and a downward spiral can ensue.) Helping children at an early stage to acquire the ability to read unfamiliar words and to pronounce them correctly gives them a feeling of control over the language and can be very empowering for them. This is especially important in French. Although a huge number of French words are phonetically regular, many words can look daunting because of strings of vowels and silent letters.

In more transparent languages such as Spanish and most of German there are no excuses. Once the sound-spelling patterns have been learned children can fly with the language, reading and spelling almost anything. They become so excited when they realise that they have this skill. Here are two examples to illustrate the difference that phonics work can make.

Sarah was a Year 11 student studying for her GCSEs. She was a very able student who was predicted As in most subjects. She was having some difficulties with her Spanish and so her parents arranged a tutor for her. During these tutorials, whenever her tutor told her a word that was new, Sarah would always ask how to spell it. It became apparent that, despite being a very able student, including in her languages, Sarah's knowledge of sound-spelling rules in Spanish was almost non-existent. This meant that she had to learn how to spell every Spanish word she knew, placing an incredible extra burden on her memory. It was a particular shame because, as Spanish is a phonetic language (you 'say what you see'), it was totally unnecessary. Sarah did, in the end, go on to get a grade A in her GCSE Spanish but others without her memory capacity will not fare as well and may get discouraged very early on.

4C were a fairly typical, keen Year 4 class learning Spanish. Their teacher, however, had spent quite a bit of time with them in Year 3, as beginners, emphasising the sound-spelling links in Spanish and they were used to reading and spelling a few simple words. One day in autumn there was torrential rain and so their teacher decided to teach them the phrase *'llueve a cántaros'* (it's raining cats and dogs). They had great fun discussing the literal meaning of the phrase – 'it's raining jugsful' – and comparing it to English phrases such as 'it's bucketing down'. Finally, their teacher got them to take out their mini whiteboards and have a go at writing down the new word *'llueve'*. Despite the tricky letters 'll' and 'v', most of the children got it right. They were so proud and it made them feel very secure in their language learning. Just imagine how they'll cope in Year 11!

» Activities for decoding words

Before the children can build up a word from the individual phonemes they must be able to hear the separate phonemes in the word, as emphasised in Chapters 1 and 2.

The particular language you are teaching will influence this activity considerably. In Spanish, because it is a phonetic language, with (almost) every letter sounded, you will be able to, and indeed need to, include words with eight, nine or even ten phonemes.

Sounds & Words – Supporting language learning through phonics

Counting Phonemes

 Before embarking on any decoding work it is worth checking that children can split a word into individual phonemes in English. Give the children some buttons, counters or multilink cubes each. Say a word clearly and slowly and ask the children to place a counter in front of them for every individual sound they hear. After you have done two or three words in English, move on to the foreign language. Start with very simple words, such as:

French	
tu	t + u = 2 phonemes
cochon	c + o + ch + on = 4 phonemes
Spanish	
me	m + e = 2 phonemes
llamo	ll + a + m + o = 4 phonemes
German	
ich	i + ch = 2 phonemes
mein	m + ei + n = 3 phonemes

If the same phoneme occurs more than once in a word you still count it each time, e.g. the French word '*été*' has three phonemes: é + t + é = été.

Below are some suggestions for words you could use. More examples are available on the recordings: **Recording: Words for Counting Phonemes** and **Resource: Words for Counting Phonemes**.

Decoding and synthesising

French

1 phoneme	2 phonemes	3 phonemes	4 phonemes	5 phonemes
eau	pin	rouge	lapin	éléphant
et	je	cinq	poisson	cheval
un	chat	poule	chapeau	dimanche

Spanish

1 phoneme	2 phonemes	3 phonemes	4 phonemes	5 phonemes
y	tú	hola	gato	noches
	me	uno	coche	limón
	sí	oso	alto	regla

6 phonemes	7 phonemes	8 phonemes	9 phonemes	10 phonemes
pájaro	amarillo	elefante	terminado	americanos

German

2 phonemes	3 phonemes	4 phonemes	5 phonemes
in	mich	meine	Katze
an	eins	Hund	prima
ob	zwei	Sonne	Pferd

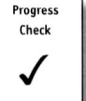

This activity will highlight any difficulties the children are having, especially understanding that sometimes a phoneme is represented by several letters. Observe them closely to see which sounds they are struggling to distinguish so that you can plan extra practice in those areas. Revisit activities in Chapter 3 to link phonemes with their spellings.

Support
Some children might benefit from having some cards with common letter strings, such as 'in', 'ch' and 'oi' (in French) to remind them that these count as one sound.

Explain to the children that this is different from the number of syllables or letters. It might be useful to compare the number of letters, syllables and phonemes in a word. For example, in French 'poisson' has just two syllables ('poi' + 'sson'), but has four phonemes ('p' + 'oi' + 'ss' + 'on') and seven letters.

In Spanish, the phonemes usually correspond to the number of letters.

Extension
The children might enjoy comparing languages. They will find it interesting, for example, to compare the French, Spanish and German words for 'elephant': '*éléphant*' (5 phonemes, 8 letters) with '*elefante*' (8 phonemes, 8 letters) or '*Elefant*' (7 phonemes, 7 letters).

Decoding and synthesising

PowerPoint Presentations

PowerPoint presentations of key phonemes have been specially devised for learners of French, German and Spanish, and are available on the CD together with PowerPoint slides for French silent letter rules and nasal sounds. During the presentations the children see and hear (spoken by you, the teacher) a series of sequences, each targeting an individual phoneme and its various possible spellings.

Note that in the interests of keeping phonics in the foreign languages fun and accessible for KS2, we have conflated a few phonemes that are very like each other and often indistinguishable although they have different IPA symbols. On the **PowerPoint presentations** children see how the phoneme is spelled, hear how it sounds when you repeat it several times and see you demonstrate how to produce the sound. Then a number of short words appear that contain the target phoneme and children can read and repeat the words. At the end of each phoneme sequence, a short sentence with many instances of the phoneme appears in a slide with an amusing illustration.

These presentations give the children an opportunity to focus on one phoneme at a time, to see the various spellings it can have and to explore it in several contexts – at letter/letter string, word and sentence levels. Seeing the short example words several times helps children to learn them as sight vocabulary which they also know how to decode, phoneme by phoneme. We advise presenting only one or a few phoneme sequences at one showing.

Support
The children can see and repeat the phoneme in a sequence as often as needed for them to feel secure with that phoneme. You can eventually have them provide as a group or as individuals the pronunciation of the sounds, words and sentences as they appear on the screen.

Extension
You may wish to encourage the children to develop their own contributions to the slides – adding more words or another sentence or two. Once the children are very familiar with the words you could use them in short spelling activities. The sentences can be used for beginner dictations of short sentences that the learners already have seen during the PowerPoint presentation.

Revisiting
Phoneme–grapheme sequences can be revisited for checking children's mastery of them and for further practice, followed by other activities in this chapter.

Decoding Word Cards

Associated with the **PowerPoint French Vowels** programmes there are follow-up word cards for children to read aloud in pairs, focusing on specific grapheme–phoneme correspondences for vowel sounds within words (see **Resource: Mini Word Cards**). The cards can be printed off – possibly on card that is the corresponding colour for that phoneme (if you have colour-coded them as suggested in Chapter 1, page 18) – and cut up. Working in pairs, the children hold up one card at a time for their partner to read aloud. The children should be encouraged to check their partner's pronunciation. You can wander around the classroom, checking on pronunciation as well.

To avoid having to cut up the cards, the whole sheet can be printed and handed out one per pair or it can be displayed on the whiteboard. Number the words so that during the pairwork one child can say a card number for the other child to read aloud.

Support
If children feel unsure about decoding whole words on their own, the activity can be carried out with the whole group in chorus. Show the PowerPoint presentation for a single phoneme again and have the children call out the words as they appear. The word card sheet could be put on the whiteboard. As you point to a word, the class can read it out.

Extension

Many children will be able to move quickly to longer words and here the lists of **Example Words by Phoneme** (**Resource**) can be used to make further word cards. Soon children can be encouraged to find other words with the phoneme, to bring in words or even to invent words.

New vocabulary

The children are encountering new words all the time, usually heard first of all but sometimes seen. Constantly draw the children's attention to the sound-spelling patterns. For example, after introducing the colours orally in Spanish but before introducing the written words, ask the children to listen carefully to the word '*rojo*' again. Can they remember which letter makes the [x] sound? Finally, show them the written word to see if they were correct.

If you have several written words on display (perhaps following a matching activity in which the children have matched the written words for pets to pictures), focus on a few of the more interesting or unusual sound-spelling links. You could even ask the children to pick out any words that look unusual or are not what they were expecting. In French, for example, when presented with the written words for pets, many children will find '*oiseau*' quite striking. If you have followed the steps in this book and done plenty of phoneme–grapheme correspondence work previously, the children should not imagine the word starts with 'wa' (as many children do when they have not been shown the French phonetic system explicitly). Even so, they will probably still find the word rather strange-looking. Talk them through 'difficult-looking' words like '*oiseau*', showing them how the sounds are built up 'oi' + 's' + 'eau'.

You cannot, of course, analyse every word the children hear or see but try to make reference to at least one sound-spelling correspondence as a normal part of most lessons. This will reinforce the phoneme–grapheme work you have done previously and keep these patterns fresh in the children's minds. The more often you point them out, the more 'normal' they will seem and patterns will start to emerge in the children's minds ("Oh yes, '*pájaro*' has a 'j' in it like '*rojo*'.").

» Pronouncing unfamiliar written words

Phoneme Boxes

An ideal time to practise decoding (working out how a word sounds from its letters) is when doing dictionary work. If the children are looking up an English word to find its translation they will need to know how to say the foreign word they eventually find. If it is a whole-class activity, once the word has been found and written on the board, for example, ask the children to discuss with a partner how they think the word is pronounced. To help, you could suggest they copy the word onto a mini whiteboard and then draw boxes around each letter, or string of letters, that they think corresponds to a phoneme. It is then just a matter of considering each letter/letter string in turn and thinking of the sound it represents. For example, the children might have been asked to find the French word for Christmas tree and the word '*sapin*' is now on the board.

Decoding and synthesising

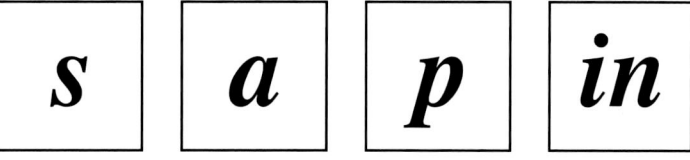

If you find some children have drawn the following:

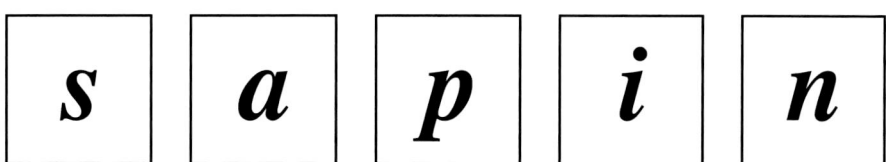

you will know that they have not identified 'in' as a typical French two-letter grapheme or digraph that represents only one phoneme. Remind them of the 'in' sound and how it is written, comparing it to words such as '*lapin*' that the children have met before. Next show them how the sounds are put together and how the whole word sounds. If several children have missed identifying 'in' it would be worth playing the **Phoneme–Grapheme Running Game** again (page 33), perhaps focusing on nasal sounds (un [œ̃], on [ɔ̃], in [ɛ̃], an [ɑ̃]).

» Silent final letters in French

Silent final letters in French can be very difficult to remember and so children need plenty of practice in recognising them when they see the written words in addition to having the rules pointed out. One activity that many teachers in France provide is to have children strike out the silent letters of single written words. This can be done on a whiteboard by using an image, for instance a cat. Show the cat and while saying the word slowly and clearly write the word '*chat*'. Point out that there is a silent letter in the word and ask the children which letter it is. They will spot the silent 't'. At that point draw a clear straight line through the final silent 't', repeating the word again and asking the children to repeat the word '*chat*'.

This striking out action is shown on the PowerPoint presentation **PowerPoint: French Silent Letters**. Large word templates are also available with the strikethrough of the silent final letters (see **Resource: Large Silent Letter Strikethrough Cards**).

Continue using images, eliciting the spoken words and then writing them out, saying them slowly and carefully so that the children can spot the final silent letters. Strike out those letters and have the children again read out the words, in chorus, in pairs to each other and possibly individually to the class. Repeat the rules for silent final consonants as you go along (see the Language support section on page 65).

Encourage volunteers to take turns at striking through the silent letter on the board. The rest of the class can make an action such as miming striking through the letter or putting their finger on their lips in a 'shhh' action. These actions can be made at any time new words come into the classroom, to reinforce the rules and remind the children.

The multisensory nature of this activity – hearing the word, seeing the strike-through and making the action – helps to reinforce the silent letters in the children's minds.

Support
The striking through of silent letters and adding a gesture are all strategies which will help children when reading and writing words in the foreign language.

Decoding and synthesising

Extension

This activity can be adapted into a game where competing teams send up individual pupils to try their luck with new words. A point is gained for correctly marking out the silent final letter(s) on the word. Include some words that have two silent letters, e.g. 'chats', and some words that do not have a silent letter at all, e.g. 'cheval'.

For pairwork practice in silent final letters in French, see **Resource: Silent Letter Word Cards,** a template for back-to-back word cards for learners to read to each other. They can check on each other's pronunciation because the back of each card shows which letters in the word are silent.

» Rhyming activities

Matching words that rhyme is a good way to practise and assess children's decoding. Deciding whether two written words have the same end sounds or rhyme is particularly useful for French because:
- there are often different spellings for the same sound;
- there are several rules about final silent letters at the end of a word.

Rhyming activities allow you to practise these aspects of the language with the children and also to assess the children's understanding of them.

Spanish and German are more transparent languages where you say virtually every letter that you see. For that reason rhymes in those languages are easier to detect.

Resource: Rhyming Pairs has rhyming pairs in the three languages.

Word card reading activities in French to practise identifying the sounds and spellings of word endings

There are many activities that you can organise around word card reading. A good example is a version of the Phoneme–Grapheme Running Game (page 33), useful for French where there are often different spellings for the same phoneme at the end of a word. Use large single grapheme cards (see **Resource: Large Grapheme Card** as a template) and stick them on the wall around the room. Each large card presents a chosen spelling of a final sound or sounds, for instance 'o' [o] or 'aire' [ɛʀ]. Hold up a large word card so that everyone can see it to read it silently to themselves, for instance, 'beau' or 'vert'. The children then run to the grapheme card that represents the final sound/s of the word, in other words rhymes with the word on the card, although the spelling might be different. You can start with just two grapheme cards and then increase the number of them gradually. Once the children are all standing at the correct poster card, they could read aloud the word on the card that you are still holding up for all to see.

Team Games

As the children become more confident of their decoding skills, this running game can be played in teams. Place a stack of smaller word cards (see **Resource: Mini Word Cards** which can serve as a template) for each team somewhere in the middle of the room. One child from each team runs to take a card from their stack, reads it silently and then runs to the grapheme card that has the end rhyme sound. The first to reach a grapheme card reads aloud the word from the card and if the decoding is correct the team gets the point. Start these activities with short words that have easily identified final sounds – that is, the final vowel sound with or without a final consonant – provided you have covered final silent letters in French (above). For instance, 'vert' and 'verte' do not end in the same sounds (do not rhyme) but 'vert', 'ver', 'vers' and 'faire' all have the same end sounds! [ɛʀ].

Decoding and synthesising

A variation is to include tricky 'odd one out' cards that do not match any of the grapheme cards. You could give an extra point for recognising that fact.

Sound Sacks with Words

With this activity the children have the opportunity not only to decode simple words but to gain confidence that they sound good in the foreign language. At the same time, with the word cards, they are developing sight vocabulary of words that they recognise and also can say correctly on sight.

The sound sacks as described in Chapter 1 (page 18) will now come in handy as children can place word cards which have the rhyming phoneme on them in (or on) the appropriate sack. The sacks may be actual bags or posters hung around the room (see **Resource: Single Phoneme Sack**), or large envelopes, that have the shortest grapheme representation of a phoneme – for instance 'o' – written on them and are stuck on the wall around the room. If you are using single small word cards (see **Resource: Mini Word Cards** to be used also as a template for other words) for three or four phonemes, you can mix them up and stack them at the front of the class. A child comes to the front, takes a card, reads it out loud and puts it in the correct sack. If the child reads it incorrectly, they can nominate another child to have a go at reading the card. This can be played as a team game, too. In this case, a team mate is nominated to read. Points can be assigned for correct decoding and correct sound sack.

If children are working in pairs they can read the cards to each other and put them in correct phoneme piles or stack them on the correct sound sack if they are using the sound sacks worksheet, available on the CD (**Resource: Vowel Sacks Worksheet b&w** and **Vowel Sacks Worksheet colour** in all three languages) also as a template for other phonemes.

Some children will want to work again and again with the same cards as they slowly build their confidence with reading aloud. You may wish to supply them with additional short words that have the target phoneme.

Support

Remind the children to read the words quietly to each other, doing some peer assessment of each other's pronunciation. They could check their Support Sheets (see **Resource: Sounds and Spellings Support Sheet**) if you are using them. The children can make a note of the sound-spelling patterns they found easiest and the ones they found tricky. Discuss any difficulties with them, either individually, if a child has been struggling, or as part of a plenary with the whole class. If, for example, several children put a particular word in the wrong sack, encourage them to explain how they came to their decision and then explain to them how to reach the right answer. Other children in the class might like to do this.

Extension

As the children become more confident you can increase the number of different phonemes (i.e. the number of sacks) and also introduce a wider range of alternative graphemes for each phoneme.

Other children may enjoy copying the words into the correct sack on the sound sacks worksheet (see **Resource: Vowel Sacks Worksheet b&w** and **Vowel Sacks Worksheet colour** in all three languages) which can also be used as a template for other phonemes. A longer word could well go into two or more sacks.

As with the sound sacks in Chapter 1 (page 18), children can be encouraged to find words at home that could go into the sacks at school.

Do these Word Pairs Rhyme?

To assess how well the children are decoding word endings, you can use **Resource: Rhyming Pairs** for some short decoding exercises (the ticks and crosses are for non-specialist teachers and should be eliminated for the children's use). Children could work in pairs if this is a practice activity or individually if you wish to assess them. You can easily shorten this test or devise other paired rhyme tests by using the lists of Words by Phoneme (**Resource: Example Words by Phoneme**) or using words you know or words from the class word bank, if you have one. Simply making an adjective feminine or making a noun plural in French will help you find out whether the children are spotting final silent letters. They do not need to know all the words to be able to decode them correctly. For instance:

Do these words rhyme with each other?

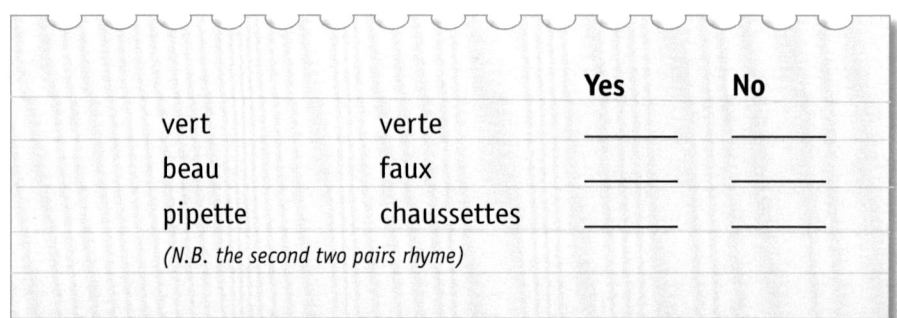

Support

A simple way of starting would be to concentrate on one phoneme, such as [o] and some of its graphemes 'o', 'ô', 'au', 'eau', 'eaux'. You would also need to add in one other phoneme, to provide some words that do not rhyme.

In another lesson you might choose to repeat the activity but concentrating on a silent final 's'. In this way, you can build up the children's knowledge of alternative graphemes and silent letters and it allows children to work at their own level. Some children will progress quickly with this and will be ready for you to start increasing the number of rhyming patterns in the activity.

Rhyming songs can be a useful and enjoyable way of identifying alternative graphemes for a given phoneme – see **Resource** and **Recording: Songs and Rhymes** for ideas.

Extension

If there are any children who are ready for a real challenge you could ask them to create their own rhyming quiz with a partner or group of classmates. If they are able to do this then you know for certain that they have understood silent letter rules and have a secure knowledge of alternative graphemes for key phonemes.

Dominoes

This activity, which children can play in pairs, small groups or teams, is played in the same way as traditional dominoes. Given a set of domino cards (see **Resource: French Domino Cards** which can be adapted to create dominoes in other languages), the children are allowed to place their dominoes where the ends of words rhyme. The game demonstrates to children the different written forms of the same sounds at the end of words. It is particularly useful for practising silent letters at the ends of words in French.

Before introducing this activity it is important to check that the children can easily decode the words on the cards. You can display the words on the board and go through their pronunciation, marking out any silent final letters. The class could read the words as a chorus and then the children could practise reading aloud the words with a partner before beginning the game.

Support
To simplify the game initially, use only three or four groups of selected cards with the same ending sound and spelling, choosing endings that should not be confusing. If children are struggling, encourage them to say the word aloud and check their pronunciation. Remind them of the sound–spelling patterns they have practised, for example in the Phoneme–Grapheme Running Game.

Extension
The activity becomes more challenging as you increase the range of endings included in the set of dominoes and introduce different graphemes for the same phoneme (such as 'au' [o] and 'o' [o] in French) and words ending in silent letters.

Children who are very secure with their decoding could be challenged to work together to create their own set of rhyming domino cards.

Rhyming Songs

This activity provides practice in identifying alternative graphemes for a given phoneme and is especially useful for work on silent final letters in French.

Before introducing a rhyming song, however, you may want to do a word-level activity to introduce some of the song's rhyming words to the children. Display the rhyming words on the board in two columns with the rhyming pairs mixed up. Ask the children to work with a partner and discuss which rhymes match up. The following example is from an invented song in French. Display these words on the board and ask the children to work out what each animal is called. Explain that the name of each animal rhymes with the word for that animal.

Support

During the pairwork go around the class listening to the discussions taking place. If anyone is having difficulty remind them to say the words aloud, quietly. Check if they are pronouncing them correctly. Draw their attention to the word *'cheval'* and ask them which name they think rhymes with it. This is the one that children usually find easiest as the two rhyming words have the same endings (*'cheval'* and *'Pascal'*). If they are still finding it difficult, narrow down the alternatives, such as 'Do you think *'cheval'* rhymes with Simon or Pascal?'

Animaux	Noms
chat	Alain
cheval	Simon
chien	Thomas
souris	Fabien
poisson	Pascal
hamster	Sophie
lapin	Robert

Once you have discussed the rhymes as a class you are ready to put them into the song (to the tune of *'Au clair de la lune'*).

As-tu un animal?

As-tu un animal?
Oui j'ai un chat
Comment s'appelle-t-il?
Il s'appelle Thomas

As-tu un animal?
Oui j'ai un chien
Comment s'appelle-t-il?
Il s'appelle Fabien

As-tu un animal?
Oui j'ai un cheval
Comment s'appelle-t-il?
Il s'appelle Pascal

As-tu un animal?
Oui j'ai un hamster
Comment s'appelle-t-il?
Il s'appelle Robert

As-tu un animal?
Oui j'ai un lapin
Comment s'appelle-t-il?
Il s'appelle Alain

As-tu un animal?
Oui j'ai un poisson
Comment s'appelle-t-il?
Il s'appelle Simon

As-tu un animal?
Oui j'ai une souris
Comment s'appelle-t-elle?
Elle s'appelle Sophie.

Extension

Children who are very comfortable with this activity can be challenged to think of other rhyming words, such as the food an animal might eat (e.g. *'riz'* for the *'souris'* and *'pain'* for the *'lapin'*). Thinking of other words will be easier for children who are in their third or fourth year of studying the language and have a wider vocabulary.

A similar song for Spanish is available (see **Resource: La Granja Extraña**).

Decoding and synthesising

Super Sentences

This activity provides the children with an opportunity to practise pronouncing a particular phoneme and also to practise saying a particular phoneme when they see its corresponding grapheme, thus building on the reading syllables activity in Chapter 3.

The sentences have been specially created to include lots of examples of a particular key phoneme. Display the sentences on the board (or copy them for the children to have in front of them) and then practise reading them aloud together as a whole class.

Try an easier phoneme to start with, gradually moving on to the 'trickier' ones (that might be more difficult to pronounce or have a very different spelling from English).

Once you have read a sentence a few times as a whole class you can then do this as a pairwork activity. This will give the children the opportunity to help and correct each other and for you to go around the class listening to pairs of children and offering guidance where needed.

Here are a couple of examples from the Spanish sentences, the second one being the more challenging:

> Tres tigres terribles ven la tele en el tren.
>
> La oveja vieja juega con el pájaro rojo.

Support

Doing this as a whole class activity means that children who are not sure can just listen and join in with the words when they are ready. As you will be reading the sentence more than once, children can join in more each time. If you want to use this activity to check if the children have understood a particular sound-spelling link you can ask small groups of children to read it aloud together. You will be able to tell if someone in that group is unable to join in or is saying the wrong thing, without having to resort to asking individual children to read it aloud, which, if they are not ready to do so, can be embarrassing and distressing for them.

Extension

Progress from shorter sentences to longer ones and from the 'easier' phonemes (that are like English) to the 'trickier' ones (that are harder to pronounce). In contrast to what has been said in the Support section above, some children will be super-confident with this activity and will enjoy the chance to read the sentence aloud individually, even faster and faster, like a tongue twister.

Follow me!

This activity builds on the children's knowledge of phoneme–grapheme correspondence, which the activities in Chapter 3 helped develop. It provides practice in matching sound to print and helps to develop their reading skills.

Choose a simple text, such as a short rhyme, and display it clearly in a large font on the board. Ask the children to follow the text, silently, while you read aloud. Stop suddenly and ask them to tell you what the next word is (to show they have followed you accurately). You can play this game several times with the same text, stopping in different places each time. The following text gives you an example of the type of text you could use and suggested places to pause (shown by /) for the first game.

Decoding and synthesising

> **C'est la poule grise**
>
> C'est la poule grise
> Qui pond dans l'église;
> C'est / la poule noire
> Qui pond dans l'armoire;
> C'est la / poule brune
> Qui pond dans / la lune;
> C'est la / poule blanche
> Qui pond sur la planche.

You can use some of the recordings of songs and rhymes (see **Recording: Songs and Rhymes**) if you prefer and simply use the pause button.

Support

Some children may benefit from having the text in front of them on their desk, rather than having to look up at the board. This will enable them to use their finger to follow the text if they wish. Also, think about where to stop and which word the children have to say. In the example above the words immediately after the pauses, which the children would have to say, are '*la*' and '*poule*', which are easy for the children to say aloud. An alternative is to ask them to come to the board and point to where you are.

Another support strategy is to stop immediately after an easily recognisable word. If there is a particularly long word in the text, try pausing straight after it. Long words tend to be easier to spot, as well as the first and last words on a line.

Your speed of delivery is also important. Pausing at the end of each line helps and also pausing more often helps the children keep their place as they don't have to follow for too long without a check.

The second time through, once the children have heard the words a few times, try stopping before '*Qui*', '*pond*' and '*dans*' to see if the children can remember how those words are pronounced. In such a repetitive poem they have heard you (or a recording) say them several times.

You might prefer to start with just one sentence, rather than a text, the first time you try this activity. Human Sentences is a great opportunity to play this. If the children have large text cards and have created a phrase or short sentence by standing in a line then you can use that sentence for this activity.

Extension

A faster delivery and longer text will challenge the children, as will going for longer between stops, so they have longer chunks to listen to. You can also try stopping before a word you want to see if the children know how to pronounce, such as '*Qui*' as suggested earlier. A real challenge for some children would be to take turns at reading the text aloud, taking over your role. (If they volunteer, this would give you a great opportunity to check their sound-spelling knowledge.)

Decoding and synthesising

» Activities for synthesising words

Synthesising is using knowledge of the phoneme–grapheme correspondences while bringing together graphemes to form syllables and then a whole word.

Building Syllables

This activity builds on the phoneme–grapheme correspondence activities in Chapter 3. Instead of linking a phoneme to a letter or letter string the children are now being asked to link two phonemes to their corresponding letters or letter strings (e.g. 'p' and 'in'). This is a middle step along the road to building whole words. It is worth pointing out to the children that they are only creating syllables, combinations of sounds, at this stage and their creations are not always supposed to make sense – although occasionally they will, by coincidence, form an actual word (e.g. *'pin'* and *'vin'* in French). Playing with sounds can be great fun and the children will enjoy creating silly-sounding syllables such as 'mu' (in Spanish).

The children can work individually, in pairs or very small groups using letter cards (see **Resource: Mini Grapheme Cards**) where each card represents one phoneme. The children must listen carefully to what you say and use the letter cards to recreate it. For example, in French if they hear 'pin' they must select cards 'p' and 'in' and put them together in that order.

As a more active variation the children could use large letters and, working in small groups, arrange themselves in order to create the syllable. A whole class variation would be to use the interactive whiteboard and ask volunteers to click and drag the letters. An exciting team variation would involve having duplicate sets of large letter cards stuck on the board or wall. A representative from each team goes head-to-head, trying to be the first to select and arrange the cards to create the desired syllable.

Following are some suggestions for syllables and the cards you would need:

Decoding and synthesising

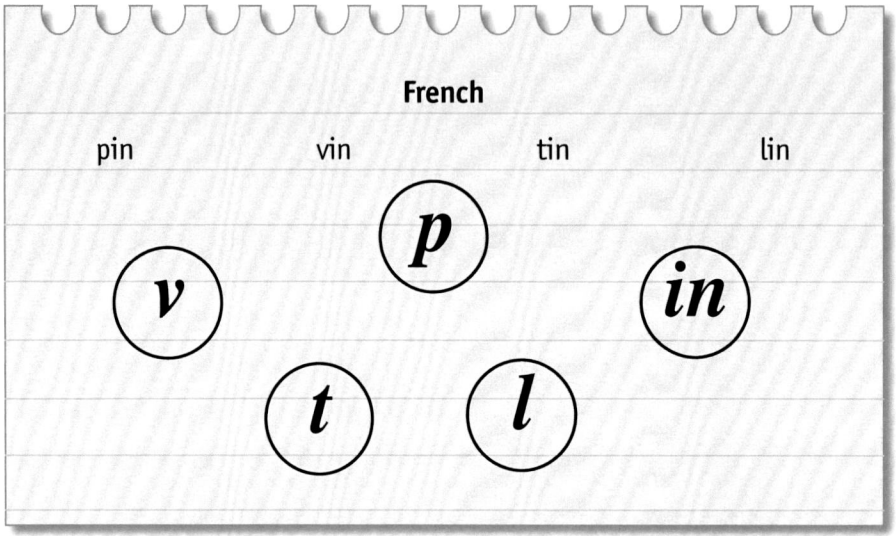

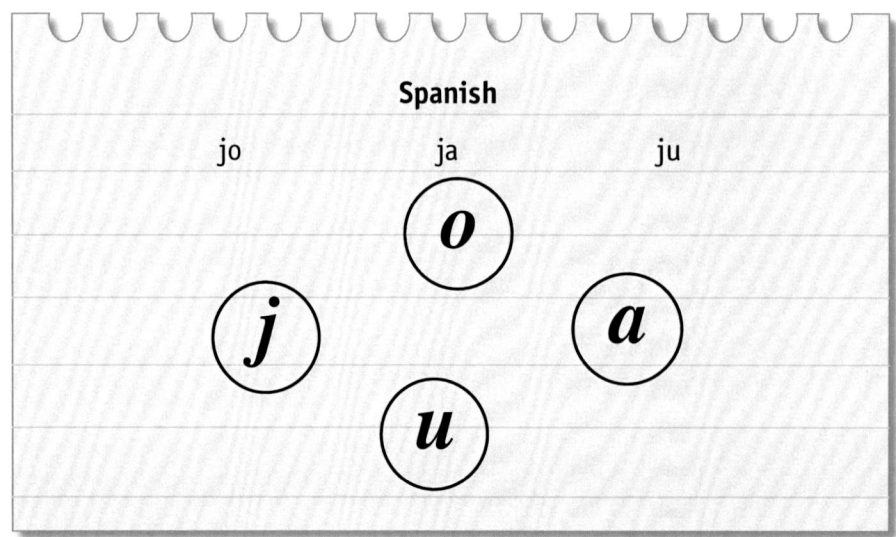

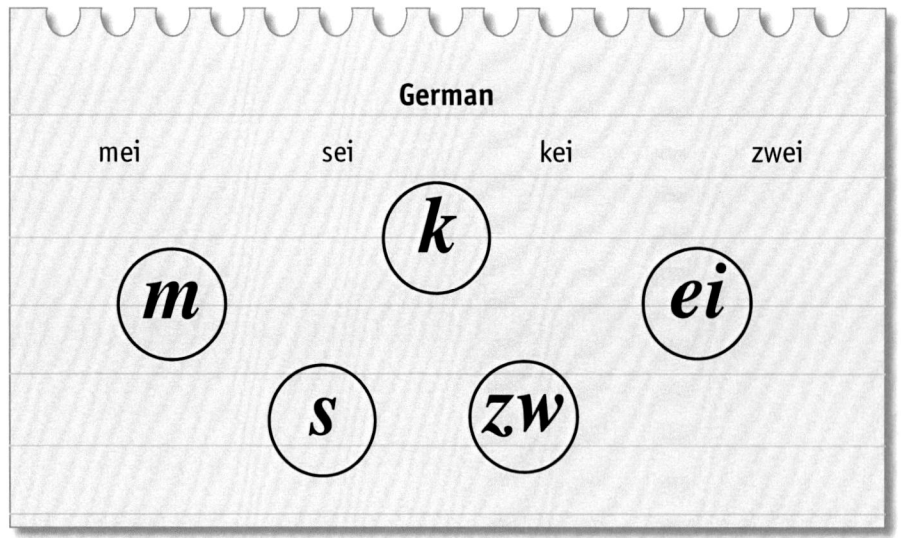

Decoding and synthesising

This activity can also be used to practise decoding skills by reversing it to practise reading syllables as in the Silly Syllables activity in Chapter 3 (page 40). Give the children the written syllables and ask them to work out how they would say them. You can then progress to giving them a string of nonsense syllables to read aloud e.g. mu, mu, mu, mu, mu and then move on to creating patterns that, when read aloud, have a rhythm to them almost like a song. Here's an example that sounds great in Spanish:

ja, ja, ja,

ji, ji, ji,

ja, ji, ja, ji,

ja, ja, ji.

Support

It is quite easy to make this activity simpler or more demanding just by choosing your phonemes carefully. Start with two sounds that are both similar to English (e.g. 'm' + 'a' = 'ma'), progressing to one similar and one different sound (e.g. in French 'l' + 'u' = 'lu') and then to two sounds that are both different from English (e.g. in French, 'j' + 'u' = 'ju'). If some children are finding this difficult, support them by saying the sounds more slowly and deliberately. Make sure all the children can hear you clearly – it is a good idea to move around the room, repeating the sound several times so no child is 'at the back'. It is also useful to take the children through some examples, showing them how the syllable is created from two different sounds. If necessary, repeat the 'Counting Phonemes' activity (page 43).

This activity is also a useful diagnostic tool. If a child is struggling with it, pay close attention to which sound/spelling combinations he or she is having particular trouble with. Are they having difficulty in distinguishing two similar sounds such as 'u' [y] and 'ou' [u] in French? Are they confusing the target language and English phonetic systems such as, in Spanish, hearing the sound made by the letter 'e' [e] and thinking of letter 'a' in English? If this is the case, revisit some of the activities in Chapters 1–3 to ensure all the 'building blocks' are in place before moving on.

Extension

Make the activity more challenging by choosing phonemes that are different from English or those representing a different sound-spelling correspondence from English e.g. 'ch' in French. Phonemes represented by strings of letters rather than a single letter also provide a greater challenge e.g. 'eau' in French.

You can also challenge the children by increasing the speed at which you say the syllables and decreasing the amount of thinking time. Adapting the activity into a team challenge would be a fun way to do this.

As the children become confident with this activity move on to two syllables together, creating a 'nonsense word', e.g. 'li-lu' or 'bé-vé'. After that it is only a short step to creating actual words.

Building words

Jigsaw Words

In this activity the children are given cards with half a word written on them (see **Resource: Jigsaw Words**). To avoid any confusion, explain to the children that you have quite simply 'chopped the words in half' and that the cards do not relate to either syllables or phonemes. Make sure that the set of cards does not include two graphemes that represent the same phoneme, especially in French, for example, in the list below, including the word *'vélo'* would cause confusion as the children would have no way of knowing whether they needed the 'o' card or the 'eau' card.

Decoding and synthesising

They must listen carefully as you say a word and then choose the corresponding cards, arranging them to create the word. Start with one- or two-syllable, phonetically regular words. Choose words that are unfamiliar to the children so that they are focusing on the sound-spelling link rather than trying to remember how they are spelled. Here is an example of possible words in French (see **Recording: Jigsaw Words**):

dindon   poule   museau   roi   lion   blaireau   bouche

Examples in Spanish and German are available on the CD (see **Resource: Spanish Jigsaw Words** and **Resource: German Jigsaw Words**).

Support
As always, start with simple words and move to longer ones with a greater variety of graphemes.

Extension
As the children become more proficient, you can reduce the number of words but split them into more parts so you get down to individual phoneme level. You will need to reduce the number of words at the same time, for example, in French: lutin, chameau, singe, lampe.

Decoding and synthesising

Missing Graphemes

This is a useful whole-class activity, which provides the children with a supportive step towards writing words phonetically. Start by writing a word on the board in large letters. Omit one of the letters or letter strings. Say the whole word aloud and ask the children to tell you what the missing letter / letter string is. For example, write the following on the board co--on and say the word 'cochon', slowly and clearly several times. The children need to supply the missing grapheme 'ch':

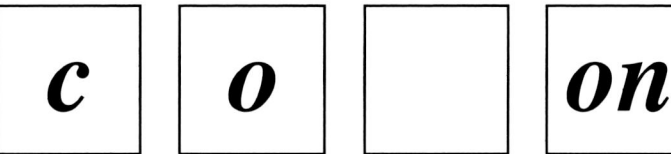

For a more active variation, give out large grapheme cards (see **Resource: Large Grapheme Card**). The child with the correct card must come out to the front and stick the card in the correct place to complete the word. This can be adapted into a team game by giving out duplicate sets of grapheme cards to each team. The first person to place the correct grapheme card on the board wins a team point.

Support
Watch the children closely to see that all are able to supply the missing grapheme/s in the word. If some are not, you can make the task easier by using shorter words with fewer overall phonemes and the activity can be carried out by pairs working together. Other formats include the interactive whiteboard and also pen and paper.

Extension

Progress to omitting more than one grapheme, e.g. 'éléphant' in French could look like this:

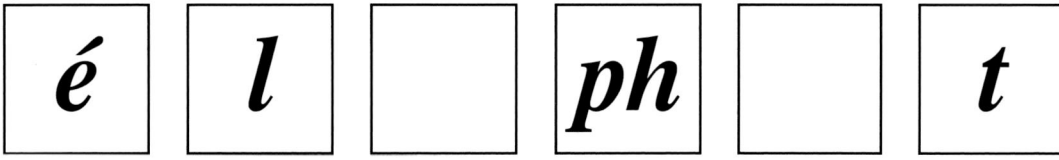

The missing graphemes are 'é' and 'an'.

Decoding and synthesising

Human Dictation

This activity is the next step from the 'Missing Graphemes' activity described above. All the activities in this book so far have been leading to this point. This is undoubtedly a form of writing, even though no pens or pencils are involved. The children select letters to form words in the same way as they do when typing on a computer keyboard. Explain this to the children so that they understand they are now writing some words, not from memory, but completely independently. This is extremely empowering for most children. In phonetic languages like Spanish this means that they should be able to write any word you say, spelling it correctly. This will come as a revelation to the children. It is something they cannot do in English, as they will know if they have weekly spellings to memorise. Even in French, whilst there will be many words with silent letters and alternative spellings for the same phoneme (such as 'o', 'au' and 'eau' for [o]) as happens in English, there are, nevertheless, a great many words that are phonetically regular and that the children should be able to write without having to learn the spelling. What a huge burden of learning that removes from the children's shoulders!

Hand out large grapheme cards (use **Resource: Large Grapheme Card**) to the children, say a word and those children with the corresponding letter cards must come out to the front and arrange themselves in the right order to create the word. Make sure, of course, that the words you choose are phonetically regular and start with simpler words with only one or two phonemes. The suggested word lists for the 'Counting Phonemes' activity at the start of this chapter may be useful, or the lists of Words by Phoneme (**Resource: Example Words by Phoneme**).

For an exciting team game, and a way of actively involving more children at once, give out duplicate sets of grapheme cards to groups of children and award a point to the first team to create the word.

Help the children to see what a 'big deal' this is. They are now starting to 'crack the code' of the foreign language. Never again will it look like a meaningless row of letters.

While the children will enjoy the kinaesthetic nature of the activity (and will love the challenge of a competitive team version), you can adapt this into a quiet, individual activity – in other words (horror of horrors!), the dreaded 'dictation'. There is anecdotal evidence that children do enjoy this, provided you start simply and ensure it is achievable. (See **Resource: Dictation Exercises**.)

One of the authors conducted a little before-and-after experiment with a Year 6 class who had done no phonics work at all. Care was taken at the outset to explain to the children that they were not expected to be able to write all (or indeed any) of the words because they had not yet learned the skills necessary to do so. The children were then asked to attempt to write a list of French words (all phonetically regular but unfamiliar to the children) as they were read out to them. The success rate, understandably, was very low amongst most of the children but it was again explained that this was of no consequence at that stage. Following several months of lessons during which there was a prominent focus on phonics including activities such as the phoneme–grapheme running game and jigsaw words, the original dictation exercise was repeated. The improvement was considerable and, in some cases, staggering, especially amongst a small group of boys who had struggled the most with the original activity.

There are two important points to note from this account. First is the dramatic improvement in accuracy apparently brought about by the focus on phonics – it 'worked'. Second is the fact that the children enjoyed the activity. They could see the progress they had made and felt a sense of achievement that they were able to write French words that were unknown to them.

Support
Start with simple words with very few phonemes such as '*pin*' in French or '*mano*' in Spanish. In French especially it is important to start with only a small range of phonemes, with which the children are familiar. As in previous activities, saying the words clearly and slowly will help.

Extension
As the children gain in confidence you can increase the number of phonemes in the word, the range of phonemes in the list and the speed of delivery. You could also include one 'bonus' word at the end of your list for those children who love a challenge.

There are lists of words for dictation available on the CD (see **Resource** and **Recording: Dictation Exercises**). The lists are arranged in increasing levels of difficulty.

The Human Stress Game for Spanish

The 'Human Stress Game' is very similar to 'Human Dictation' above, with the difference that you are focusing on stress. This activity is particularly important in Spanish where there are clear rules governing syllable stress and written accents that are used to show any deviations from these rules. (For an explanation of Spanish rules of stress, see page 73.)

Once the children are standing in a row and have correctly formed a word (see 'Human Dictation' above), ask them to listen carefully as you say the word several times. As you say it, really emphasise where the stress falls. Ask the children to listen and decide which part of the word is stressed (it will be a syllable, rather than an individual phoneme). The children with the corresponding letter cards take a step forward.

Support
Recording: Words by Syllable Count and **Resource: Words by Syllable Count**.

The simplest way to begin is by playing the syllable clapping game (see Chapter 1, page 23) and get the children to stamp their feet on the stressed syllable, e.g. in Spanish, the word '*elefante*' would be as follows:

e (clap), le (clap), fan (clap and stamp), te (clap).

In Spanish, when you start to talk to the children about written accents, a useful example is the name *Jose*, or *José*. Explain there are two variations of this name, let them hear the difference (and clap and stamp them out) and then write the words on the board to let them see the difference.

Crazy Phrases

Once children are able to use their knowledge of phoneme–grapheme correspondence to write phonetically regular words they can move on to phrases. At its simplest level this activity is only a small, yet important, progression from writing dictated words. Moving from a list of words to a phrase allows the children to see and hear how the language fits together. When composing their own phrases there will be other factors to consider, such as word order and adjectival agreement, which are beyond the remit of this book. The children will have to combine their knowledge of the phoneme–grapheme correspondences with other knowledge about the language they are studying.

You could dictate some very simple phrases, such as '*Le coucou fou*'. The children can also have fun composing their own. For example, you could ask them to think about rhyming words and to choose some creatures who might be friends with each other. Possible pairs include:

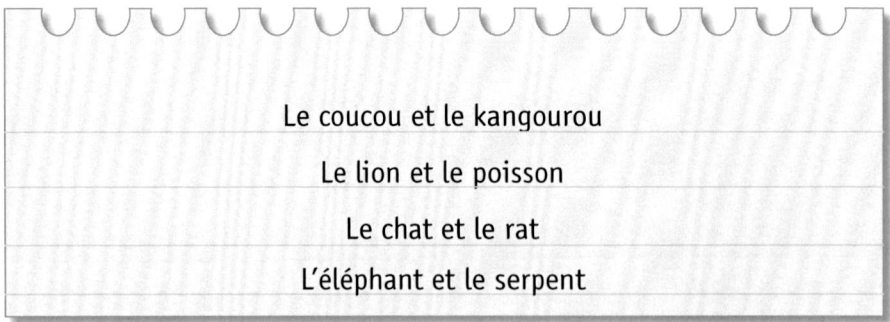

Le coucou et le kangourou

Le lion et le poisson

Le chat et le rat

L'éléphant et le serpent

They could also try combining an animal with an adjective that rhymes, such as: *L'éléphant méchant*, or *Le chameau gros*.

Support
With dictated phrases you can differentiate the level of difficulty of the phrases. Simplify the phrases by including only one key phoneme per phrase and choosing easier phonemes (that are easier to hear and are similar to English), e.g. *Le chat de Papa*.

The sound banks described in Chapter 1 would be a useful support for the children when starting to compose their own phrases. You can also help them by discussing beforehand some useful words and steering them towards phonetically regular words.

Extension
Dictated phrases can be made more challenging by making them longer, mixing several different phonemes and including 'harder' phonemes (such as nasal sounds) and silent letters.

Decoding and synthesising

Sensational Sentences

The next step is to move on to whole sentences. Being able to write whole sentences can be very exciting and empowering for the children. They can suddenly feel as if they can 'do' the language. By working with sentences rather than single words the children will start to hear the rhythm of the language, where the stress falls, what happens to the intonation and, sometimes, they will hear liaison between words.

As with the phrases, the children will now need to combine their knowledge of phonics with other language skills, such as agreements and word order. With sentences they will also have to deal with verb endings and will need particular support in this area (see below).

Moving to creating sentences does not have to be a big step. With a short phrase containing a noun and an adjective (similar to those in the last activity), simply swap the adjective for a verb and you have a very simple sentence, for example in French: *Le cheval marche*, or *Le poisson glisse*.

Adding another noun, as the object of the sentence, opens up many more possibilities for creativity, e.g. *Le chat déteste le rat* or *La vache porte une jupe*.

Sentences can be built up further by adding adjectives and/or adverbs, e.g. *Le serpent rose avale un chou énorme*.

As with the phrases, you can ask the children to write sentences they hear (listening to you or to a sound file on the computer). All of the examples above consist of phonetically regular words and could be written using knowledge of the phoneme–grapheme system of the language. The most fun comes, of course, when the children get to compose their own sentences.

Support
The dictated sentences can be differentiated easily by altering the length, the speed of delivery and the mix of phonemes. The difficulty level will also be affected by aspects such as the particular phonemes included, liaison and silent letters.

With their own compositions, support the children in the same way as for the phrases. You will also need to help them tackle verbs. The simplest way to start is with a core collection of -er verbs in the third person. The following are examples of some that the children should be able to write using their phoneme–grapheme knowledge:

joue (plays)	glisse (slides)	marche (walks)	avale (swallows)	porte (wears)

chasse (chases)	adore (loves)	déteste (hates)	trouve (finds)	regarde (looks at)

and some slightly harder ones:

mange (eats)	nage (swims)

Decoding and synthesising

Extension

With their own creations challenge the children by asking who can create the longest sentence, the funniest sentence or the sentence containing the most occurrences of a particular phoneme. They could begin with the super sentences for reading. (See **Resource** and **Recording: Sentences to Read Aloud**.)

This would also make a good I.T. activity. The children can work individually or in pairs at a computer, perhaps listening to a sound file of a sentence (which can be of differing levels of difficulty, suited to each child), which they then type on the screen. This allows the children to listen to the dictated sentence as many times as they need to. (Sound files of sentences are available on the CD.) They could then add some artwork to create a poster, e.g. *Le coucou fou joue avec le kangourou roux.*

By the end of this chapter most children should be able to read aloud phonetically-regular words, pronouncing them accurately. They should also be able to read aloud short phrases and simple sentences that are composed of phonetically-regular words. They should be able to match sound to print, listening to a spoken text and following the written version. They should also be able to say whether two written words rhyme.

Some children may be operating with a smaller repertoire of phonemes. When matching sound to print they may need a slower delivery and when reading aloud they may be more comfortable with very short sentences.

Other children may be confident with a very wide range of phonemes, alternative spellings and silent letters. They may be able to read aloud longer sentences fluently and confidently and be able to match print to speech delivered at normal speaking pace.

In terms of writing, most children should be able to use their knowledge of phoneme-grapheme correspondences to write phonetically-regular words. They will be able to build short phrases and simple sentences that are made up of phonetically-regular words.

Some children may still need support such as grapheme cards and will be comfortable with very short words containing only a few phonemes (e.g. *lapin*). They may be able to build very short phrases made up of such words.

Other children may be able to write longer words containing a greater number and variety of phonemes (e.g. *dimanche*). They may be able to write longer sentences accurately, demonstrating a knowledge of issues such as written accents and silent letters.

We have progressed through the book from single phonemes and graphemes to whole sentences. This is not a stand-alone scheme of work but rather a resource to awaken awareness in the teacher of the importance of building up children's phonics knowledge and their aural, oral and written skills and to help teachers with their own knowledge and skills while developing the children's. We hope you've enjoyed the journey.

» Language support

In this chapter we present – in the **Key Phoneme Guides** that follow – the most important sounds in each language that are often very different from English. Rules for pronunciation, spelling, accents, intonation and stress are given in each language section. The information is for you, the teacher, so that you have an overview of the phonology of the language and a quick reference section.

You can use it to support your own CPD with the foreign language. It can provide a framework for planning the phonology sections of your FL teaching. It will be useful for tracking what you have covered with the children, and what you need to monitor and possibly revisit. It will frame the progress the children are making towards building a whole phoneme–grapheme system for themselves which they can rely on so that they do not need to resort to English alone when listening, speaking, reading, writing or learning vocabulary in the foreign language. Although English can be helpful in support of learning, when children 'put on their French – or Spanish or German – thinking caps' we hope that they are as well knit as possible!

Some sounds are very similar in English and French, Spanish or German. These are mostly consonant sounds like /m/ or /n/. These sounds can be transferred from English, i.e. said as you would do in English.

Some sounds are new, not made when we speak in English, and they have to be practised with their lips, tongue, teeth, palate and throat – LTTPT – in different positions than are used for speaking English. The mouth has to move more, particularly in French.

The main vowel sounds in French, Spanish and German sound very similar in these three languages and they all need more mouth movement than is required for English.

The children will need to learn to form the new sounds with their LTTPT. The accompanying CD will show how to do it. It can be good fun but needs to be monitored and practised until making the sounds becomes automatic and fluent.

In each language-specific section the vowels are presented in the order 'a-e-i-o-u' including variations and additional sounds that appear in the language. Then we present consonants which have different spelling-sound links from what we are used to in English. The sounds that do not appear here can be transferred from English without distorting too much the native pronunciation – remember that there are all sorts of regional variations in all the languages, including English! We aim for a roughly acceptable conventional pronunciation of French, Spanish and German here.

To present the sounds of the language we have used symbols of the International Phonetic Association (IPA) because after long thought, discussion and trials, we feel that they best present the sounds in a simple, clear and consistent way. We have based our IPA symbols and transcriptions on what appears in the Collins Robert French Dictionary, the Collins Klett and Langenscheidt German Dictionaries and the Collins Spanish Dictionary, all of which we have used throughout.

If you wish a more detailed approach to pronunciation, please refer to a dictionary which has phonetic transcriptions of each word. Study the list of phonetic symbols at the front of the dictionary, but note that phonetic transcriptions of the sounds of a word may differ slightly from what a particular native speaker expects. Even two phonetics experts may transcribe the same sound somewhat differently. Certainly there can be alternative pronunciations of the same word as spoken by different native speakers of the language. In addition, dictionaries may have slightly different phonetic transcriptions for the same sound. The Collins Robert French Dictionary we used, for instance, based their phonetic transcriptions on 'standard Parisian'.

The presentation of the spellings, sounds, and pronunciation

For each of the three languages you will find the following format for the presentation of the Key Phoneme Guide. First, the written letter or letter string in the language appears on the far left. These show how the sound is spelled.

Then the International Phonetic Association symbol or symbols for the sound appear in brackets [ ].
If there is a similar sound in English we then offer it between two forward slashes / /. Sometimes an English word then appears which contains that sound or something very similar to it. For some sounds there simply is no English equivalent.

We then give an example word in the language to help you hear how to make each key phoneme on the CD.

A support sheet for each language with the sounds and their spellings is available (see **Resource: Sounds and Spellings Support Sheet)** for printing out as a poster and/or for individual pupils to have as an A4 sheet for themselves. The organisation of the support sheet is similar to the Key Phoneme Guide in this chapter, but simplified for easier access by the children, probably in Years 5 and 6.

Please note that on the **Sounds and Spellings Support Sheets** we have often conflated long and short vowels. If a child remarks that he or she hears long and short vowels, or you have taught them, simply agree that there are such in the language. For instance, for the sake of easy reference for French we have put all the 'a' sounds together on the suppport sheet, whether long or short. The purpose of the **sheet** is for quick reference for decoding and for spelling in the foreign language.

Silent letters sections

Silent letters are a familiar phenomenon for young readers of English and so the children should be able to grasp easily that there can be silent letters in the foreign language. The rules for silent letters are fairly straightforward in French, Spanish and German.

However, children will notice that **digraphs** (and polygraphs) – letter strings which represent only one sound – sometimes seem to have 'silent' letters. Such graphemes should be taught and learned as chunk spellings for one sound, as we teach them in this book. Here are some examples:

In French:	In German:
eau – [o]	ei – [aɪ]
aux – [o]	ie – [i]

Information and rules about silent letters for French, Spanish and German are included in each of the language-specific sections of this chapter.

Accents, stress and intonation

These areas are presented in each language-specific section for that language. In some cases brief explanations are given about accents where the children might find it interesting to know, for instance, what an umlaut in German actually represents (an 'e') and consequently what it does to the vowel sound.

We hope you find the following sections useful.

Sounds & Words – Supporting language learning through phonics

» Key Phoneme Guides

French

Vowels

Be careful not to make your French vowel sounds into diphthongs, i.e. two or more gliding sounds. Vowels are single, clear sounds in French which don't really have approximations in English. Please listen to the accompanying recording for the **Key Phoneme Guides** (**Recording: Individual Phonemes**) to hear the pronunciations.

a	[a]*	bateau
a, â	[ɑ]*	pas

* Although these are officially separate sounds (i.e. they have different phonetic symbols) they are often virtually indistinguishable in everyday speech, and in **PowerPoint** presentations and on the **Sounds and Spellings Support Sheet** we have grouped them together

è/ai/ei/et	[ɛ]	mère
é/-er/-ez	[e]	été
e	[ə]*	je
eu	[ø]*	deux

* Whilst these are officially separate sounds (i.e. they have different phonetic symbols) they are often virtually indistinguishable in everyday speech and in **PowerPoint presentations** and on the **Sounds and Spellings Support Sheet** we have grouped them together

eur	[œ]	fleur
i	[i]	il
o/au/eau	[o]	bateau
o	[ɔ]	gomme
ou	[u]	douze
u	[y]	lune
oi	[wa]	moi

Nasal vowels – concentrate on the nose

un	[œ̃]	pronounce the 'œ' sound while pinching nose, mouth a bit rounded
on	[õ]	pronounce the 'o' sound while pinching the nose, mouth nice and round
in	[ɛ̃]	pronounce the 'ɛ' sound while pinching the nose, remember to smile!
an	[ɑ̃]	pronounce the 'a' sound while pinching the nose, remember to drop your jaw!

Language support

Consonants – most are like English with a few exceptions; 'h' is silent

ç/ss	[s] /s/	the same pronunciation as for the letter 's' in English
s	[z] /z/	the same pronunciation as for the letter 'z' in English
j/g (e,i)	[ʒ]	as in 'vision'
ch	[ʃ] /sh/	like the English 'shush' sound 'shh!'
r	[ʀ] /ghrr/	as in the growl 'ghrrr!', drop jaw slightly, place your hand on throat to feel it
qu	[k]	the same pronunciation as for the English letter 'k'
gn	[ɲ] /ny/	as in the English word 'canyon'
ill	[ij] /eeyuh/	like the French vowel 'i' with a little follow-on; remember to smile!

Important digraphs

-er/-ez [e]   marchez

The very common French word endings -er and -ez are actually digraphs for a single sound which is the same sound as the ending -é in French.

Accents in French

The French accents ´ and ` change the sound of the letter 'e':

le – [lə]

lé – [le]

lè – [lɛ]

Because these sounds are difficult to equate to any English sounds, we propose that you consult the pronunciations for e, é, and è on the CD.

The cedilla accent on 'c' means that it is pronounced as a single 's' [s].

The accent ^ does not affect pronunciation. It sometimes indicates a lost letter 's'. Once children know this it can be fun to put up a new French word for them to guess the meaning, for example:

forêt – forest
château – castle
hôtel – hostel

Silent letters in French

Six important and useful **rules** are given here about silent letters in French which you might wish to explain or teach the children.

Rule 1:

The letter 'h' is usually silent: 'hôtel' [otɛl]

There are some exceptions to this which you may note as they arise.

Rule 2:

The following vowels/consonants are silent when they appear at the end of a word:

'e', 'p', 'd', 't', 's', 'z', 'x', 'es'.

These final silent consonants may be combined with each other, so for instance, in the word 'chats' both the 't' and the 's' are silent: [ʃa].

Rule 3:

The letters 'r' and 'z' after 'e' at the end of a word are silent, as shown in 'Important digraphs' above. These silent letters turn the otherwise silent 'e' into an 'é' [e] sound, for example in: 'manger' and 'mangez' which rhyme with 'marché'.

We suggest simply explaining that after an 'e' final 'r' and 'z' are silent. Children in their third or fourth year of study may be interested in noting how '-er' and '-ez' could be thought of as a consistent digraph for the [e] sound with the 'r' and 'z' silent letters, as noted above about digraphs.

In France children are sometimes taught to remember silent final letters by changing their colour or by marking a line through them. See **PowerPoint presentation: French Silent Letters**

Ma tortue ne marche pas vite

Elle aime manger de la salade.

Elle est contente ...
       mais toujours très lente!

NOTE 1: in poetry and songs the final 'e' may be pronounced as a schwa or 'uh' [ə] sound. Congratulate the children who notice this and say it is special for French poetry and songs to link sounds between words together to make a smooth rhythm.

NOTE 2: in spoken and sung French there is usually a liaison effect between the final consonant, whether it is **normally** sounded or is silent, in one word and the following word if that word starts with a vowel:

ils ont – (the letter 's' makes a 'z' sound) [il zō]
vs
ils vont – (the letter 's' is silent) [il vō]

Note that the final letter 't' is, as always, silent in these two examples.

Rule 4:

The rule for 'u' after 'g' and 'q' is that it is always silent (with a few rare exceptions):

qui – [ki] /kee/

guignol – hard 'g' [giɲɔl] /geenyoll/ (the 'g' is pronounced as in the English word 'gate')

Rule 5:

A final silent 'e' preserves the preceding consonant sound that, if it were the final letter, would normally be silent. This silent 'e' can indicate the feminine form:

vert – [vɛʀ] /vair/

verte – [vɛʀt] /vairt/

Explain to the children that 't' as a final consonant is normally silent but, once you add an 'e' at the end, the 't' is no longer the final letter, so it is no longer the final silent letter. The 'e' is!

Rule 6:

And last but not least difficult: the ending '-ent' for the 3rd person plural present tense form of a verb is silent!

(ils/elles)	aiment	[ɛm]	/em/
(ils/elles)	marchent	[maʀʃ]	/marsh/
(ils/elles)	trouvent	[tʀuv]	/truv/

Remember: The 's' of 'ils' and 'elles' always forms a liaison with a following verb that begins with a vowel:

ils aiment – (the letter 's' is pronounced like 'z') [il zɛm] /eelzem/

Intonation in French

Intonation in French gives the stress on the final syllable. In phrases and sentences the stress falls on the final syllable of what Collins Robert call a 'sense group', i.e. a group of words that form an idea or section of a sentence. So, in a short sentence the stress is on the final syllable of that sentence: 'Viens i**ci**!' (stress is noted in bold).

The voice falls at the end of a French sentence.

Questions have a slight rising tone at the end.

Sounds & Words – Supporting language learning through phonics

Spanish

Vowels

a	[a]	gato
e	[e]	tele
i	[i]	gris
o	[o]	coche
u	[u]	azul
y	[i]	y

Semi-consonants

i, y	[j]	Like the English 'y' as in 'yet'	hielo
u	[w]	like the English 'w' as in 'win'	huevo

Diphthongs – these are actually two short letters blended

ai / ay	[ai]	like the English 'i' as in 'slide'	hay
au	[au]	as in 'cow'	aunque
ei, ey	[ei]	like the English 'ay' as in 'day'	rey
eu	[eu]	take the sounds for 'e' and 'u' and say them together, quickly. It is a little bit like saying the English word 'oh' with an exaggerated 'posh' accent!	euro
oi, oy	[oi]	like the English 'oy' as in 'toy'	voy

Consonants

b	[b]	this is the same as letter 'v' in Spanish. At the start of a word or after 'm' or 'n' it is pronounced like the English 'b' as in 'boy'.	banco
b	[β]	in all other positions it is like saying a 'b' without letting your lips touch (there is a very slight vibration)	había
c	[k]	before 'a', 'o' and 'u' it is like the English 'c' as in 'cat'	calle
c (e/i)	[θ]	like the English 'th' in 'think' (This is the same as the Spanish 'z'.)	cinco
ch	[tʃ]	like English	chico
d	[d]	at the beginning of a word and after 'l' or 'n' it is like 'd' in English	dice
d	[ð]	in other positions it is like the English 'th' in 'although'	nada

Language support

g (e/i)	[x]	before 'e' or 'i' it is the same as the Spanish 'j'	**generoso**
g	[g]	before other letters it is like English 'g' in 'go'	**gracias**
h		always silent	
j	[x]	this is similar to the 'ch' in the Scottish 'loch'	**julio**
ll	[ʎ]	similar to the English 'lli' in 'million', although in many regions it is pronounced like the English 'y' as in 'yes'	**llave**
ñ	[ɲ]	similar to the English 'ni' as in 'onion'	**año**
qu	[k]	like the English 'c' in 'cat'	**que**
r	[r]	this is trilled like the Scottish 'r'. You really need to come from Glasgow to manage this one! Try saying 'drink' with a Scottish accent. (At the start of a word and after 'l', 'n' and 's', a single 'r' is pronounced like 'rr')	**pera**
rr	[rr]	'rr' (or a single 'r' if it is at the start of a word or after 'l', 'n' or 's') is trilled even more strongly	**perro**
s	[s]	this is usually pronounced as the English 's' in see, except in the instances given below	**solo**
s	[z]	before 'b', 'd', 'g', 'l', 'm' and 'n' it is pronounced like the English 's' in 'nose'	**desde, mismo**
v	[b]	this is the same as letter 'b' in Spanish. At the start of a word or after 'm' or 'n' it is pronounced like the English 'b' as in 'boy'.	**verde**
v	[β]	in all other positions it is like saying a 'b' without letting your lips touch (there is a very slight vibration)	**nieva**
z	[θ]	like the English 'th' in 'think' (This is the same as the Spanish 'c' before 'e' or 'i'.)	**zumo**

Spanish stress rules

One of the great things about Spanish is that there are very clear rules about which syllable to stress in a word. This means that you always know how to say any new words you come across.

If a word ends in a consonant (except 's' and 'n') you stress the final syllable, e.g.

    ciu**dad**   doc**tor**   pa**pel**   co**lor**   a**zul**

If a word ends in a vowel, as the vast majority of Spanish words do, or 's' or 'n', you stress the penultimate syllable, e.g.

    man**za**na   **blan**co   ga**lle**ta   tra**ba**jan   **ga**tos

Why 's' and 'n'?

You will notice that 's' and 'n' are associated with plurals in Spanish ('s' to make nouns plural and 'n' to make the 3rd person of a verb plural). If you consider a noun such as '**ga**to', once you make it plural it no longer ends in a vowel but you still want the stress in the same place (you don't want it to become 'gat**os**'!). Having 's' and 'n' as exceptions avoids a lot of written accents (see below), including almost every plural noun in Spanish.

Written accents

Whenever there is a deviation from the rules Spanish makes it clear by using a written accent ´ (note that this is different from many languages, such as French, where a written accent changes a letter's sound).

    E.g.   **plá**tano   (without the ´ it would be 'plat**a**no')

            árbol   (without the ´ it would be 'ar**bol**')

            an**dén**   (without the ´ it would be '**an**den')

A written accent is also used to distinguish two words that are spelled the same (there is no room for ambiguity in Spanish!), e.g.

        tu (your)   tú (you)

        mi (my)   mí (me)

        el (the)   él (he)

        solo (alone)   sólo (only)

        esta (this)   está (is)

        si (if)   sí (yes)

(note that when an accent is on the letter 'i' you don't write the dot)

So, in answer to the question that children often ask, 'Does it really matter?', you can explain that it does or else you might end up saying something entirely different altogether, e.g.

    inglés (English)   ingles (plural of the word for groin)!

You might also notice that the 'question words' have written accents in direct questions, so 'cuándo' in the sentence '**when** will he arrive?' but 'cuando' in the sentence 'he always brings flowers **when** he arrives'.

Sounds & Words – Supporting language learning through phonics

Diphthongs

Note that if you are a beginner in Spanish you may prefer to leave this section for a while.

Diphthongs are two vowel sounds that are blended together to make a single sound (and therefore a single syllable). In Spanish they occur when you have one weak and one strong vowel together.

The strong vowels are 'a', 'e', 'o'; the weak vowels are 'i' and 'u'.

The Spanish diphthongs are:

>   **ai** (or **ay**)
>   **au**
>   **ei** (or **ey**)
>   **eu**
>   **oi** (or **oy**)

Please refer to **Recording: Individual Phonemes** for a pronunciation guide.

In Spanish, written accents are used to split a diphthong so that you know to pronounce each vowel separately, e.g. 'país' (without the accent this would be a one-syllable word, rhyming with 'ice' in English. With the accent it becomes a two-syllable word, with the stress on the second syllable).

Diphthongs are also created when you have two weak vowels together, 'iu' or 'ui', for example:

fuimos (two syllables) (the 'u' is a semi-consonant here, almost like 'w' in English)

viuda (two syllables) (the 'i' is a semi-consonant here, almost like 'y' in English).

Diaeresis

Spanish does have another written accent, the diaeresis – two dots, over a letter 'u': ü. This means that the 'u' should be pronounced (it is used in cases where the 'u' would normally be silent).

Silent 'u'

A letter 'u' is always silent after 'q'. 'qu' is pronounced like 'k' in English.

A silent 'u' is also sometimes used after a 'g' as a kind of buffer to keep the 'g' hard before 'e' or 'i'. Remember that 'g' is pronounced like English 'g' (as in 'gate') before 'a', 'o' and 'u' but before 'e' and 'i' it becomes like the Spanish 'j' [x] (pronounced like the 'ch' in Loch Ness), for example:

sigue	(follow)	(pronounced 'see-gay')
guisantes	(peas)	(pronounced 'gee-san-tays') The 'g' is pronounced as in the English word 'gate'
but		
pingüino	(penguin)	(pronounced 'pin-gwee-no') As the 'u' is between the 'g' and 'e' you would normally assume it is there purely in its role as buffer and you would not pronounce it. However, the diaeresis over the 'u' tells you that it should be sounded.

Sounds & Words – Supporting language learning through phonics

German

Vowels

There are long and short vowels **a, e, i, o, u, ä, ö, ü** in German.

We can safely say that although there are long and short vowel sounds in German, they are simply variations of each other. The LTTPT are more relaxed with the short vowels. It is useful to recognise and produce long vs short vowels because they aid in spelling German.

Decoding and spelling tip

In written German the vowel is long when it appears before a single consonant or before an 'h' with or without another consonant after it. Short vowels appear before two consonants (except 'h'). There are very few exceptions to this rule. To get a sense of the difference between long and short vowel sounds, try:

long	long	short
Rad	fahren	Ratte
Esel	sehr	essen
Schule	Schuh	jung

It's quite easy!

In the **Key Phoneme Guide** that follows, long vowel phonemes are shown with the symbol ':' after them. Short vowels appear without that symbol and are a moderately shorter version of the long vowel sound, for instance, the jaw is not dropped quite so low for [a] as for [ɑ:].

Avoid making diphthongs of the single vowel sounds, whether long or short, i.e. say 'ahh' and not 'ahh-uh'.

A few phonemes and phonetic symbols have been omitted from this list. We have followed Collins Klett and Langenscheidt dictionaries to decide this.

NOTE: all German nouns begin with a capital letter!

In the list of vowel sounds below, the long vowel sounds come first followed by the short vowel sounds. Listen to the audio recording **Recording: Individual Phonemes** for the pronunciations.

Vowels

a	[ɑ:]	as in 'father'	**Vater**
	[a]		hast
e	[e:]		zehn
	[ɛ]*	as in 'let'	**essen**

* [ɛ] is found more commonly in German dictionary transcriptions than [e] for the short 'e' sound; it is also used for the short 'ä' sound below

ä	[ɛ:]		**Mädchen**
	[ɛ]	as in 'let'	**Wäsche**
-e	[ə]*	as in 'the'	**Katze**

* The [ə] (called 'schwa' in phonetics) is the final sound of every German word ending in 'e' like 'rote', 'weisse' and the 'e' sound in the word endings: -en, -er, -es, -el, -em.

Language support

Sounds & Words – Supporting language learning through phonics

i	[iː]	as in 'meet' teeth nearly closed, wide smile	**ihn**
	[i]	smile more relaxed	**mit**

o	[oː]	very rounded lips	**ohne**
	[ɔ]	lips less rounded than for [oː]	**oft**

ö	[øː]	tightly rounded lips with upper lip pulled down over the upper teeth	**böse**
	[œ]	upper lip not pulled down so far	**öffnen**

u	[uː]	tightly rounded lips	**gut**
	[u]	lips less tightly rounded	**Mutter**

ü, y	[yː]	make a tight circle of the lips and pull the upper lip down over the upper front teeth like a rabbit. This will take practice as we don't make this movement in English.	**über**
ü	[y]	the circle made by the lips is less tight, upper lip less tightly pulled down over teeth	**fünf**

Diphthongs – two blended vowel sounds:

ei, ai	[aɪ]	as in 'eye'	**Mai**
au	[au]	as in 'house'	**Maus**
eu, äu	[ɔʏ]	as in 'boy'	**neun**

Important digraphs

Two digraphs have **no exceptions** but they can easily be confused by the children. These may need special attention given to them:

ie	[i]	similar to, but slightly shorter than, the 'ee' in 'tree'	**sieben**
ei	[aɪ]	as in 'eye'	**eins**

Language support

Sounds & Words – Supporting language learning through phonics

Consonants

Most German consonants are spoken crisply at the front of the mouth, often right behind the teeth. The list below is of grapheme-phoneme correspondences that are *different* from English.

ch	[ç]	a kind of hissing shushing sound made by pressing the sides of the tongue to the roof of the mouth and pushing air out through the tunnel this makes behind the teeth with the mouth slightly open	**Kirche**
ch	[x]	a guttural sound made at the back of the mouth near the throat; slightly rounded lips, jaw slightly dropped	**ach**
g	[g]	a hard 'g' (except in a few borrowed foreign words)	**Gold**
j	[j]	as in 'yes'	**ja**
ng	[ŋ]	as in 'sing'	**singen**
r	[r]	frontal 'r', could be trilled or just flapped. Practise using 'dr' or 'tr' to get the tongue flapping behind the teeth	**trinken**
ß/ ss/-s	[s]	hissing sound an ß represents two 's's one on top of the other but is no longer used in German orthography although still seen in older printed material. Children who have been to Germany will have seen it and may ask about it.	**essen**
s	[z]	buzzing 'z' sound	**reisen**
v	[f]	English 'f' sound	**vier**
w	[v]	English 'v' sound	**Wiedersehen**
z, tz	[ts]	as in 'cats'	**Platz**
sch	[ʃ]	/sh/ as in 'shop'	**Schule**
sp	[ʃp]	/shp/	**spielen**
st	[ʃt]	/sht/	**stehen**
pf	[pf]	**pf** needs practice at the front of the mouth to join the sounds neatly together	**Pferd**
zw	[tsv]	**zw** needs practice at the front of the mouth behind the teeth to join the sounds together	**zwei**
-ig *	[ç]	soft 'g' sound or almost 'ch' as Scottish 'loch' * This ending has many different pronunciations throughout the German-speaking world. It can be said as [k] or [ʃ], for instance.	**vierzig**
qu	[kv]	**qu** needs practice to join the sounds together	**Qualle**

Note: **r** [ʁ], a rasping 'r' at the back of the throat, is not a sound made in English; the Collins Klett Dictionary we used does not include this sound in its list of German phonetics. Although children might want to try to learn this sound or may be able to bring the making of it from another language they know and they could be encouraged to do so, we do not include it as being absolutely necessary here.

Language support

Sounds & Words – Supporting language learning through phonics

Umlauts

The word 'umlaut' means changed or changing sound. An umlaut over a letter changes the sound of that letter. Originally the two little dots of the umlaut was the letter 'e' and it followed the vowel. Then the 'e' was written above the vowel. Then the 'e' became the two dots that are used today:

fuer → fu̇r → für

If you haven't got umlauts on your keyboard you can still spell any word correctly by inserting an 'e' after the letter that should have an umlaut:

Maedchen fangen Maeuse mit Kaesestueckchen. (Girls catch mice with cheese bits.)

Mädchen fangen Mäuse mit Käsestückchen.

Silent letters in German

There are no silent letters in German **except** for the silent letter 'h' in the German digraph 'th':

th   [t]   /t/   Theater

Stress and intonation in German

The syllable that is usually stressed in a German word is the word stem, often the first or sometimes the second syllable: **seh**en, **komm**en, Ka**nin**chen.

Many prefixes are stressed: **Wieder**sehen, **auf**stehen, **aus**trinken

Questions end on a rising tone. Sentences always end on a falling tone.

In a long German sentence the voice rises before the comma, and then falls at the end of the sentence.